THE FATHER'S KISS

Validation Through Affirmation

Dr. Gregory L. Cruell

Copyright © 2018 Dr. Gregory L. Cruell.

All rights reserved. No part of this book may be reproduced, stored, or transmitted by any means—whether auditory, graphic, mechanical, or electronic—without written permission of the author, except in the case of brief excerpts used in critical articles and reviews. Unauthorized reproduction of any part of this work is illegal and is punishable by law.

This book is a work of non-fiction. Unless otherwise noted, the author and the publisher make no explicit guarantees as to the accuracy of the information contained in this book and in some cases, names of people and places have been altered to protect their privacy.

ISBN: 978-1-4834-8479-2 (sc)
ISBN: 978-1-4834-8478-5 (e)

Because of the dynamic nature of the Internet, any web addresses or links contained in this book may have changed since publication and may no longer be valid. The views expressed in this work are solely those of the author and do not necessarily reflect the views of the publisher, and the publisher hereby disclaims any responsibility for them.

Any people depicted in stock imagery provided by Getty Images are models, and such images are being used for illustrative purposes only. Certain stock imagery © Getty Images.

Lulu Publishing Services rev. date: 5/9/2018

Scripture quotations taken from the Amplified® Bible (AMP), Copyright © 2015 by The Lockman Foundation Used by permission.

Scripture taken from the King James Version of the Bible.

Scripture quotations marked (NIV) are taken from the Holy Bible, New International Version®, NIV®. Copyright © 1973, 1978, 1984, 2011 by Biblica, Inc.™ Used by permission of Zondervan. All rights reserved worldwide. www.zondervan.com The "NIV" and "New International Version" are trademarks registered in the United States Patent and Trademark Office by Biblica, Inc.

Scripture quotations marked MSG are taken from THE MESSAGE, copyright © 1993, 1994, 1995, 1996, 2000, 2001, 2002 by Eugene H. Peterson. Used by permission of NavPress. All rights reserved. Represented by Tyndale House Publishers, Inc.

Scripture quotations marked ISV taken from The Holy Bible: International Standard Version is Copyright © 1996-forever by The ISV Foundation. ALL RIGHTS RESERVED INTERNATIONALLY.

Scripture quotations marked (NLT) are taken from the Holy Bible, New Living Translation, copyright ©1996, 2004, 2015 by Tyndale House Foundation. Used by permission of Tyndale House Publishers, Inc., Carol Stream, Illinois 60188. All rights reserved.

Scripture quotations marked (TLB) are taken from The Living Bible copyright © 1971. Used by permission of Tyndale House Publishers, Inc., Carol Stream, Illinois 60188. All rights reserved.

Scripture quotations are from the ESV® Bible (The Holy Bible, English Standard Version®), copyright © 2001 by Crossway, a publishing ministry of Good News Publishers. Used by permission. All rights reserved.

Scripture taken from The Voice™. Copyright © 2012 by Ecclesia Bible Society. Used by permission. All rights reserved.

Acknowledgements

To the Author and Finisher of my faith, my heavenly Father, and Jesus Christ my Lord and Savior. You "kissed me" with your grace and saved me when I did not know what grace was and I am eternally grateful!

To my beloved wife Deirdre. God "kissed me" again when He gave you to me as my wife for life. Your friendship, love and encouragement for almost 40 years has blessed me more than words can express. Know that I love you and I always will. To my sons and daughters, children and grandchildren, a continued manifestation of The Father's Kiss in my life. You are a royal priesthood, a chosen generation. Never forget your heritage and legacy in Christ and in our family.

To the countless members of the family of God that I have had the privilege to serve the Lord with in over 36 years of ministry. We laughed together, cried together, and prayed together. Our God-centered fellowship and relationships have been *The Father's Kiss* of His grace and I will remember you always.

To my pastors, Bishop Nate and Valerie Holcomb. Almost 30 years ago Deirdre and I were "kissed by God" when we first met. Our children and our children's children, have also been "kissed by God" because of you. Bishop, thank you for the impartation of the Father's Kiss upon me as a son. Your impartation illuminated this God breathed revelation that will go into eternity with everyone that receives the grace of The Father's Kiss.

xvii - First two paragraphs
pg. 41 - Last paragraph
pg. 52 - Paragraphs 2-3
pg. 54 - Paragraph 2
pg. 58 - Paragraph 2-4
pg. 58 - Last paragraph
pg. 97 - 2nd paragraph

Contents

Acknowledgements vii
Preface xi
Chapter 1: What Is The Father's Kiss? 1
Chapter 2: What The Father's Kiss Is Not 16
The Father's Kiss is *Not* Entitlement 16
The Father's Kiss *Is Not* Manipulation 18
The Father's Kiss *Is Not* A Fleshly Imitation 21
Chapter 3: The Character of The Father's Kiss 26
The Image of Christ 27
The Substance of the Image 28
The Authority of the Ring 32
Chapter 4: You Have Not Many Fathers (Mothers) 36
Chapter 5: The Father's Kiss Validation
Through Acceptance 43
The Pleasure and Purpose of the Father 43

Adopted By The Father 47

Validated and Accepted By the Father 52

Chapter 6: The Father's Kiss Validation
Through Affirmation 57

Affirmation is the Voice of the Father 57

Affirmation is The Inspiration of the Holy Spirit .. 63

Affirmation Is Aspiration By the Holy Spirit 65

Affirmation Is The Validation of Sons Through
Failure 69

Chapter 7: Why Every Son (Daughter)
Needs a Father 76

Protection and Direction By Correction and
Instruction 77

The Influence of Social Media On Our Sons and
Daughters 84

Chapter 8: The Hope of the Father's Kiss 93

The Hope of The Father's Kiss 94

Chapter 9: The Legacy of The Father's Kiss 101

Learning From the Past, Living In the Present,
Building For the Future 101

Epilogue 113

Preface

This book is a story of validation, reconciliation, and affirmation that is embedded in the grace of God. Pastors, leaders and members of the Body of Christ, this book is for all of us; *The Father's Kiss-- Validation Through Affirmation*.

The revelation of *The Father's Kiss* was given to me as I was sitting in a barber shop in Junction City, Kansas waiting to get my haircut; as I recall the year was 2003.

As a young boy of about 8 or 9 years old was getting down from the barber's chair after getting his haircut, a gentleman walked over (which I assume was the boy's father) to assist him in getting down from the chair.

After brushing a few hairs from the boy's shoulders, the father then bent over and *kissed* the young boy on his forehead. As I watched this scene unfold with tears in my eyes, at the age of 45, I remember wanting what that young boy had just received from his father;

I had a desire to be *kissed* by my Father; this was the genesis of *The Father's Kiss*.

The first time I experienced *The Father's Kiss* was from my spiritual father, Bishop Nate Holcomb, Christian House of Prayer Ministries, Killeen and Copperas Cove Texas. The impartation of *The Father's Kiss* from my spiritual father was a confirmation and activation of the revelation I had received in the barber shop in 2003. It was the Apostle Paul that said to us as the people of God that we were to *"greet one another with a holy kiss"* (Romans 16:16 King James Version).

When my spiritual father kissed me on the cheek, I experienced the veracity and integrity of *The Father's Kiss*; a *holy kiss!* The word *holy* in Romans 16:16, carries the meaning of sanctification, or the manifestation of the character of *"holiness"* revealed in personal behavior, conduct and actions.

To be clear, the substance of the *Father's Kiss* is *agape*, the unconditional love of God the Father that is an impartation of His *holiness* with no trace or elements of *worldliness*.

A kiss that we may give or exchange with family, or members of our church community is ***natural;*** rooted in Paul's admonishment to the church at Rome. *"Love one another with brotherly affection [as members of one family], giving precedence and showing honor to* *one another"* (Romans 12:10 Amplified Version). Paul admonished the church at Rome to love one another with both *"phileo"* (brotherly) and *"storge"* (family) love.

In this book, we will discuss how **The Father's Kiss** is both natural and spiritual. Natural from the perspective that as envoys and representatives of **The Father's Kiss** we are human beings. Spiritual from the perspective that there is an impartation of **God's Spirit** of holiness from *"fathers to sons."*

1 John 3:1-2 says, *"Behold, what manner of love the Father hath bestowed upon us, that we should be called* **the sons of God**. *Therefore, the world knows us not, because it knew him not.*

Beloved, now are we **the sons of God**, *and it doth not yet appear what we shall be: but we know that, when he shall appear, we shall be like him; for we shall see him as he is."* (King James Version)

Not only are we *called to be the sons* of God—it is ***who we are***, *as the sons of God*. To be called a son of God has nothing to do with gender but has everything to do with looking like Christ. Galatians 3:28 reminds us, *"there is neither Jew nor Gentile, neither slave nor free, nor is there male and female, for you are all one in Christ Jesus"* (New International Version).

The first time that I witnessed **The Father's Kiss** bestowed upon a congregation was in 2006 at Crossroads Christian Church Dover Delaware, Pastors Anthony and Margo Wallace. After preaching a Father's Day message entitled, *"A Ring and A Kiss."* I then watched Pastors Anthony and Margo Wallace bestow upon members of their congregation **The Father's Kiss**, both naturally and spiritually.

I stood in awe of God's grace and manifested presence in **The Father's Kiss** as I watched the manifestation and impartation of the Holy Spirit's ministry released at the altar that day. The altar call must have lasted over an hour, but nobody left the service that day until they had received the **Father's Kiss** from their spiritual father, Pastor Wallace!

The second time that I was able to experience and see the manifestation and impartation of the **Father's Kiss** was at New Life Church in Cleveland Mississippi, Bishop Roderick and Pastor Mary Mitchell.

As it had been at Crossroads Christian Church in Dover Delaware, so was it at New Life Church in Cleveland Mississippi. After preaching the message entitled, *"A Ring and A Kiss,"* members of the New Life Church waited patiently at the altar to experience the manifestation and release of **The Father's Kiss** by their spiritual father, Bishop Roderick Mitchell.

The backdrop for this book is one of the most well-known stories in the Bible in that of the Prodigal Son in Luke's Gospel, chapter 15:11-24. Although we see the error of the son's way's, the greater truth of this story is the love of the father for His son as revealed in ***The Father's Kiss*** (vs.20).

The Father in this story represents God, our heavenly Father and the son represents us as God's people, the Body of Christ. After a season of *"riotous living"* which means loose, reckless, wild, extravagant living, the son spent all that he had and went quickly from prosperity to poverty.

With no money and no means to take care of himself, the Message Bible says in verse 17-18 that, *"he signed on with a citizen there who assigned him to his fields to slop the pigs. He was so hungry he would have eaten the corncobs in the pig slop, but no one would give him any. That brought him to his senses. He said, 'All those farmhands working for my father sit down to three meals a day, and here I am starving to death. I'm going back to my father."* In the 20th verse the Bible says, *"when he was still a long way off, his father saw him. His heart pounding, he ran out, embraced him, and **kissed him**."*

The original Greek translation of the word kissed is *"kataphileō,"* which means to *"kiss passionately, earnestly."* [1] This is the perspective of this book. ***The Father's Kiss*** is a passionate, earnest embrace of His love for us as His people. It is this love that validates

---
[1] Strong, James. *Strong's Concordance.* Austin, TX: WORD*search*, 2007. WORD*search* CROSS e- book.

the fact that there is nothing that we could ever do to make God love us, and there is nothing that we can ever do to make God not love us!

As the people of God, we have been robbed of receiving and experiencing **The Father's Kiss** and many are not even aware that the crime has occurred! **The Father's Kiss** validates, confirms, reconciles, restores, and renews once and for all, God's passionate, earnest love for us!

The subtitle of the book, **Validation Through Affirmation**, is to draw our attention to God the Father *validating* Jesus the Son by the strength of *affirmation* as seen in Matthew 3:16-17 (King James Version). *"And Jesus, when he was baptized, went up straightway out of the water: and, lo, the heavens were opened unto him, and he saw the Spirit of God descending like a dove, and lighting upon him.*

And lo a voice from heaven, saying, **this is my beloved Son, in whom I am well pleased**." And in Matthew 4:1, *"then was Jesus led up of the Spirit into the wilderness to be tempted of the devil"* (King James Version). The phrase *"I am well pleased"* in this passage means to *think well* of, to *approve*.

In its original Latin root, the word validate means to be *"strong, effective, or powerful."* It can also mean, *"support the truth or value of."* Affirmation in its original etymology means *"to make steady or to strengthen."*

In the context of Matthew 3:17, we see the power of *validation* and *affirmation* in the life of Jesus. Jesus was being led by the Spirit of God into the wilderness to be tempted, tested and tried by the devil!

Knowing what was before His Son, God *affirms* (*makes steady and strengthens*) and *validates* (*makes effective, powerful, valued and supported*) Jesus by saying this is my beloved Son in whom I am well pleased! *If Jesus as the Son of God was validated and affirmed in His life, how much more do we as God's people need the same!*

Some may need more affirmation than others, and others not much at all. Yet, the point I am making is that if Jesus as the Son of God needed to be affirmed in life and ministry, *we will need to be affirmed also.*

As Christians we know that the love of God for us as His people is real, yet there are still times in life where hardships, difficulties, trauma and drama plague us. Scars of the past desire to control our present and alter our future in Christ.

Although the prodigal son came to himself, recognized and repented of the mistakes and mishaps that sought to destroy him, the love (*symbolized by the kiss*) of his Father was greater than his past, and the son was restored.

The International Standard Version of Luke 15:21-24 says, *"then his son told him, 'Father, I have sinned against heaven and you. I don't deserve to be called your son anymore. But the father told his servants, 'Hurry! Bring out the best robe and put it on him and put a ring on his finger and sandals on his feet. Bring the fattened calf and kill it, and let's eat and celebrate! Because my son was dead and has come back to life. He was lost and has been found.'* **And they began to celebrate."**

As it was for the prodigal son thousands of years ago, my prayer is that we will receive and apply the revelation of **The Father's Kiss**, in our heart, home, church, community and workplace and party like we never have before, and dance as if nobody is watching!

As we do so, I believe the revelation of **The Father's Kiss** will be the catalyst that ignites a celebration and transformation in us and the people around us (family, friends, co-workers) that personifies Jesus exhortation in John 8:32, *"And ye shall know the truth, and the truth shall make you free"* (King James Version).

Chapter 1: What Is The Father's Kiss?

"So he returned home to his father. And while he was still a long way off, his father saw him coming. Filled with love and compassion, he ran to his son, embraced him, and kissed him" (Luke 15:20 New Living Translation).

As we begin to answer the question of this chapter, there are four elements in the passage above that are central to the nature of *The Father's Kiss*. For most of us as Christians the context of this parable gives us insight concerning the actions of the prodigal son. However, I submit that this parable is more about the *love of the father* for the son, than the sons' nature as a prodigal. In the passage above, we see the nature and character of the father for his son in his:

1. *Love*
2. *Compassion*
3. *Embrace*
4. *Kiss*

} Luke 15:20

The word love is recorded 310 times in the King James Version of the Bible. The only type of love that the father had for his prodigal son was *"agape."* Naturally, love maybe defined as *"a strong affection for another rising out of kinship or personal ties, physical attraction or affection."* There is love between a parent and child, brothers and sisters, or love given by a person to an animal or object. It basically comes down to the fact that everyone inevitably either loves something or someone.

Further, love is a motivator and gives us the reassurance that we will be cared for and helped in times of need. The Message Bible translation of 1 John 4:7-8 says, *"My beloved friends, let us continue to love each other since love comes from God. Everyone who loves is born of God and experiences a relationship with God. The person who refuses to love doesn't know the first thing about God, because God is love—so you can't know him if you don't love."*

In the preceding passage in the original Greek, there are two forms of the word love; *agapē* and *agapaō*. These two words are used primarily in the NT to describe the attitude of God toward His Son and humanity. These two words further express the essential nature and character of God and His love which is *unconditional*. Love can be known only from the actions it prompts. It was *agape* (unconditional love) that the prodigal received when he came back to his father's house.

Agape is born of the character and nature of God which is spiritual and not natural. When Jesus said in the King James Version of Luke 6:27, *"love your enemies, do good to them which hate you,"* the word that Jesus chose for love is agape. It was not *"phileo"* (brotherly love) or *"storge"* (family love).

Jesus said that we are to love even our enemies with *agape, the unconditional love of God*! Our world is full of hurting people and if we live long enough, we will discover that hurting people hurt people.

When recording artist Dionne Warwick recorded her song, *"What the World Needs Now is Love,"* in April 1965, what many people do not know is that the lyrics Hal David wrote focused upon what God gives us.[2] The expressions and sentiments of this song remain the same today. When people do not experience God's love, there is a void or vacuum that is created in that person's life and character. And in the words of Dionne Warwick, *"what the world needs now, is love sweet love. It's the only thing that there's just too little of."*

When one person mistreats or abuses another person the cycle of abuse and misuse many times continues and is passed on from one generation to the next. When a person has not experienced agape

---

[2] http://americansongwriter.com/2009/12/chicken-soup-for-the-soul-behind-the-song-what-the-world-needs-now-is-love/. Accessed February 11, 2018.

love, the God kind of love, they can never express with others what they have not experienced. Thus, the proverb, *"hurting people hurt people."*

Although the son had disrespected and disregarded his father and life circumstances had left him abused and misused, when he came to himself and went back to his father's house he was greeted with *agape*, and compassion from the father.

Compassion means to literally "suffer together with another and a desire to alleviate the suffering." An embrace in this context means *"to hold someone closely in one's arms, especially as a sign of affection."* It is the compassion and embrace of God for us as sons and daughters that brings us to the subject of this book; **The Father's Kiss.**

As stated in the preface, the original Greek translation of the word kissed is *"kataphileō,"* which means to *"kiss passionately, earnestly."* The parable of Luke 15 shows us the Father's (God's) passionate love for humanity (prodigal son) which is seen in His compassion, embrace, and loved expressed by a *kiss*. Another way to view the essence of this parable is the reality of **God's grace, reconciliation, restoration and validation through affirmation** of the son communicated by **The Father's Kiss**.

The New Living Translation of 2nd Corinthians chapter 5 says, *"anyone who belongs to Christ has become a new person. The old life is gone; a new life has begun!* [18] *And all of this is a gift from God, who brought us back to himself through Christ. And God has given us this task of **reconciling** people to him.* [19] *For God was in Christ, reconciling the world to himself, no longer counting people's sins against them. And he gave us this wonderful message of **reconciliation**."*

The word reconcile in the original Greek means, *"to change, or exchange."* Hence, of persons, *"to change from enmity to friendship, to exchange wrong for right, to bring back together."* Regarding the relationship between God and man, reconciliation is what God accomplishes, exercising His grace towards us, His unmerited favor. **The Father's Kiss** is a tangible expression of God's grace endowed upon us both naturally and spiritually because **the Father wants to reconcile with us!**

To empower simply means, *"to give power or authority to; to entitle and enable."* The authority that the prodigal had recklessly and wastefully given away, **The Father's Kiss** empowered; or gave power and authority back to the son.

To restore literally means to *"give back"* that which existed before. To *re-establish,* returning to the ultimate ideal and plan for man as established in the Garden of Eden (Genesis 1:26-28). The emphasis of restoration is *separation* from the former, negative influences of life to enjoy what is forward; which is restoration.

The Father's Kiss give's back, restores what has been lost. Reconciliation *exchanges wrong for right and brings back together that which has been separated.* After living his life for a season in self-centered indulgences, the Bible says that when the prodigal came to himself, he went back to his father's house (Luke 15:17).

Through all that had transpired in his life, the good the bad and the ugly, when he got back to his father's house by the endowment and impartation of **The Father's Kiss**, there was *grace, restoration, reconciliation, validation and affirmation* for the son by the love of his father (Luke 15: 22-24).

When Paul in Romans chapter 16:16 said to *"greet one another with a holy kiss,* a holy kiss is of the same nature of validation, affirmation and love as noted in the conversation above. A *holy kiss* has nothing to do with one's *sexuality* but has everything to do with the *reality* of the love of God expressed between born again believers (John 3:3).

As the body of Christ, we have been robbed of the ability to greet one another with a holy kiss, which is an element of God's grace and love for His church. It is important at this point to reiterate and note the distinction between **"The Father's Kiss"** as seen in Luke 15:20 and the Apostle Paul's **"holy kiss"** of Romans 16:16.

THE FATHER'S KISS

The Father's Kiss is both *natural* and *spiritual* in nature. Utilizing Paul's principle of 1 Corinthians 15:46, *"the spiritual does not come first, but the physical does, and then comes the spiritual"* (New International Version). From this principle or biblical truth, we can rightly deduce there is a *natural kiss* and a *spiritual kiss*.

For the purposes of this book, the Apostle Paul's *holy kiss* represents that which is *natural* and can be exchanged amongst members of the body of Christ. The *Father's Kiss* is *spiritual* in nature because it is in representation of God the Father. The question that naturally follows from this discussion is who can release or impart ***The Father's Kiss*** if it is spiritual in nature?

In Luke 15:20 the father kissed ***his son***. Paul's *holy kiss* in Romans 16:16 was an admonition for a *holy kiss* to be given to any and everyone in the body of believers. Yet, the ***Father's Kiss***, in representation of a manifestation of God, can only be given to a ***son*** (***daughter***) by a *"spiritual father."* *"For even if you had ten thousand others to teach you about Christ, you have only one spiritual father."* (1 Corinthians 4:15 New Living Translation).

Paul was the pastor of the church at Corinth, but he was also their spiritual father. Many, if not all the members of the church at Corinth came to the

Lord through Paul's ministry. From this truth it is important that we recognize and know that every *spiritual father is a pastor but not every pastor is a spiritual father*. Furthermore, you do not become a spiritual father overnight.

It is a long, arduous journey of resiliency, overcoming hardships and being steadfast in faith and growth in God before one can be seen as a spiritual father. What God has called the pastor to do is well known in the King James Version of Jeremiah 3:15, the Bible says, *"and I will give you pastors according to mine heart, which shall feed you with knowledge and understanding."* In other words, a pastor is to feed and lead, or provide knowledge and understanding of God's will and ways for His people.

A pastor functioning in the truth of Jeremiah 3:15 will never have to tell the people that he leads, that I am your spiritual father. The people will tell their pastor, that *I see you* as my spiritual father!

The only reason that Paul had to remind the church of Corinth that I am your spiritual father is because of their immoral behavior and conduct. They were not simply spiritual children to Paul but *beloved* spiritual children (1 Corinthians 4:14) and in need of instruction and correction.

Spiritual fathers set the example of godliness for spiritual sons and daughters through their own life.

Spiritual fathers don't just teach or preach—their *life becomes a message from God*; *"declared to be the epistle of Christ ministered by us, written not with ink, but with the Spirit of the living God"* …. (2 Corinthians 3:3 King James Version).

Paul became this manner of *epistle* to Timothy when he reminded him, *"But you have observed my doctrine, manner of life, purpose, faith, tolerance, love, and patience"* (2 Timothy 3:10 King James Version). Through the course of their relationship, spiritual father to spiritual son, Paul placed his mantle of leadership upon Timothy as his son in the faith.

To the church at Corinth on one occasion, Paul says, *"Wherefore I beseech you, be ye followers of me. For this cause have I sent unto you Timotheus, who is my beloved son, and faithful in the Lord, who shall bring you into remembrance of my ways which be in Christ, as I teach everywhere in every church* (1 Corinthians 4:16-17 King James Version).

In 2nd Kings chapter 2, Elisha watched Elijah be carried up into heaven in a whirlwind. As Elisha continued to watch, he cried out, *"My father! My father!"* A declaration of God as his heavenly father, and the prophet Elijah as his spiritual father. (2nd Kings 2:13 King James Version). The mantle had been passed from Elijah to Elisha and the assignment as a spiritual son received.

Elisha would not have been able to do what God had commissioned him to do without the teaching of his spiritual father Elijah as a mentor, model, and motivator.

The son in Luke's parable needed his father both *naturally* and *spiritually* and when he came to himself recognized that everything that he needed, was in his father's house. There was a void in his life, both naturally and spiritually that only by being reconciled to his father could he be made whole.

One of the greatest tragedies that we are experiencing today is not only do we have lost son's, but we also have **fathers that are lost**. Like many men in our society today, I grew up without the love of my natural father. The story of my family is that my grandfather left my grandmother when my father was still in the sixth grade.

In that day and time, the mindset was you don't need to go to school, you're the oldest boy so you must get a job and work to take care of the family. Therefore, my father grew up without the love of his father and could not give to my sisters and I love that he had never known. I'm grateful that in his later years my father experienced an endowment and impartation of God's grace of reconciliation for himself.

A question that may naturally arise from this aspect of our conversation is **why do men need The**

Father's Kiss? Here's a response that I trust will answer this question.

From the time that men are little boys, if as a boy you fall and scrape your knee, everyone around you says, "get up from there and don't you cry because big boys don't cry!"

The fear was real because if as a young boy people saw you cry, they would call you a punk, a sissy and many other derogatory terms that as a young boy you did not want to be associated with your name!

Consequently, growing up in an environment like this, young boys grow up into teenagers and on into manhood with this same manner of thinking. In other words, instead of *expressing* what was going on internally, there is a *suppressing* of life's challenges and difficulties that a young boy or man may be currently experiencing.

An inability to effectively communicate with a wife or children is a direct result of an inability to understand authentic relationships. A very simple definition of relationship means, **relate- to- me- on- my ship**!

Our public-school education, from kindergarten through high school, never lays the foundation to experience authentic relationships. There are no classes in this process that teach us how to establish relationships of trust, and environments of grace.

In this season of life for most of us, it was a fight for survival in some shape, form or fashion. From fights on the streets to *fights* in the classroom, trying to learn and understand why going to school is so important. To relate to someone on their ship is to *"seek to first understand before you yourself are understood."* What this further means is *"that I give up my right to be right"* as I seek to first understand a person before I try and impose what I think upon them.

The reality is that *I am not* that person; I have not had the life experiences that person has had and if we are going to have *effective* authentic relationships, we must first seek to understand others, or relate-to- them- on- *their*- ship.

It is essential in this light that we know that everybody has a story and that story is uniquely theirs. I came across this poem some years ago that says: *"Your life is writing a story. A chapter each day by the deed's that you do, by the words that you say. People will read what your life writes whether faithless or true. What becomes your life story is really up to you."*

Millions of children grow up without their biological fathers and without the balance of both a father and mother in the early stages of life and they are thrust into a lifetime of being disadvantaged.

Many of the statistics that we read, or review provide us with story after story of abandonment and abuse from many fathers. And this is certainly true, however it is ***not true*** for all fathers.

Depending upon some of the research that you may discover some fathers would say, "I knew that my children could do better than me and that is the reason why I left." Others would possibly respond with statements like, "I could no longer take the abuse that I received from your mother." In the world in which we live today it is not simply men abusing women, but ***women are also abusing men!***

By no means am I making excuses or condoning fathers that have left their children. However, what that man needs is ***The Father's Kiss***.

His life story, where and how he grew up are factors in his current story of abandonment of his children. What this man and men like him need is an endowment and impartation of God's grace on and in his life as expressed by ***The Father's Kiss*** of grace, reconciliation and restoration.

When the father kissed his son in Luke's parable, it was a sign and symbol that ***you can*** and ***you will do better this time!*** The father because of his love for his lost son, refused to allow his sons life story to end in disaster due to poor choices and mistakes.

The prodigal in the parable had made some mistakes, and to be clear, all of us have made mistakes in life; but it never changed the fact of the Father's love for us! There is nothing that I've ever done to make God love me and there is nothing that I can ever do to make God not love me.

When the son came to himself, everything that he was experiencing *externally* (life in the pig-pen), *internally* he came to know that there was a solution to his problem. Which he believed that now that I'm back in my father's house, there's a new end to my story and my story begins again with an endowment and impartation of God's grace of reconciliation and restoration which is **The Father's Kiss**.

"A man does not need to be flawless to be a perfect father because love never fails (1 Corinthians 13: 13 King James Version)."

Main Points: What Is The Father's Kiss?

- The Father's Kiss is the agape love of God that is unconditional.
- The Father's Kiss is the manifestation of God's grace and empowerment of reconciliation and restoration.
- Reconciliation means *to change from enmity to friendship, to exchange wrong for right.*

- All of us have made mistakes in life; but it never changed the fact of the Father's love for us!
- To empower is *to authorize, entitle and enable.*
- A *holy kiss* has nothing to do with one's *sexuality* but has everything to do with the *reality* of the love of God for us all (Romans 16:16). Paul's *holy kiss* is *natural* and can be exchanged amongst members of the body of Christ.
- The Father's Kiss is *spiritual* in nature because it is in representation of God the Father himself (Luke 15:20--1 Corinthians 4:15).

Chapter 2: What The Father's Kiss Is Not

In chapter 1, we discussed the make up or nature of what the Father's Kiss is. And now, I believe it is just as important to establish what *The Father's Kiss Is Not*.

The Father's Kiss is **Not** *Entitlement*

My father was an extremely good provider and hard worker. His uncommon work ethic was attributed to the standards he learned while growing up in the South. He was taught that hard work would always pay-off, and that no one owes anyone anything. I am so grateful that he instilled a good work ethic in my siblings and me.

Born in the late 1950s, growing up in the '60s and '70s, my parents insured that I had a vivid understanding of overcoming limitations without an attitude of entitlement. I remember only having three television channels: ABC, NBC, and CBS! All television programming ceased in that era at 11PM with the national anthem being played and the American flag waving in the wind.

Today cable networks advertise 300 to 500 channels that stream into our homes, 24/7. There are those in our modern-day society that feel like they have to have it all! Perhaps with the attitude, "It's my right." Through television, radio, social media and the internet, we are exposed to a barrage of materialistic and entitlement viewpoints that many times creates a mindset that says, "somebody owes me!"

A basic definition of entitlement is, *"the belief that one is inherently deserving of privileges or special treatment."* Although the prodigal in Luke's parable lived a privileged life, it was not due to entitlement; it was because of the father's love! When the son came to himself, he said, *"I will arise and go to my father, and I will say to him, Father, I have sinned against heaven and before you. I am no longer worthy to be called your son. Treat me as one of your hired servants"* (Luke 15: 18-19 King James Version). At this point in his life, the son exhibited a heart of *repentance* and not *entitlement*.

We cannot say the same for Absalom, the beloved son of King David. According to 2nd Samuel 13, Absalom fled from Jerusalem after having his brother Amnon killed for raping his sister Tamar. Although he spent three years in Geshur, Absalom never forgave his father for not punishing Amnon for his offense against his sister. Absalom had acquired a heart of *entitlement*—as a matter of fact, he thought he would make a better king than his father!

In 2nd Samuel 14, Joab, the general of David's army knew the king longed to have Absalom back home. So, he convinced a woman of Tekoa to talk with the king about bringing the banished Absalom home. As the account goes, Absalom was brought back to the kingdom, but he was not repentant. Absalom was possessed by a mindset of entitlement. He believed he deserved privileges and special treatment because he was a son of the king. Tragically, Absalom was snared by the devil's trap of *manipulation*.

The Father's Kiss Is Not *Manipulation*

"Then Joab arose, and came to Absalom unto his house, and said unto him, wherefore have thy servants set my field on fire? And Absalom answered Joab, Behold, I sent unto thee, saying Come hither, that I may send thee to the king, to say, wherefore am I come from Geshur? It had been good for me to have been there still: now therefore let me see the king's face; and if there be any iniquity in me, let him kill me. So Joab came to the king, and told him and when he had called for Absalom, he came to the king, and bowed himself on his face to the ground before the king and

*the king **kissed Absalom**"* (2nd Samuel 14:31-33 King James Version).

David's kiss was a kiss of *reconciliation* while Absalom carried with him a mindset of *manipulation*. After returning from Geshur, Absalom was denied access to the palace and the king for two years.

Therefore, he devised a plan to be fully reconciled with his father, but it was not *reconciliation* that was the makeup of his deceitful heart, but rather *manipulation*. Absalom knew if he remained barred from the palace and his father's presence, he would never be considered a possible heir to the throne.

To manipulate is to *"have control over others by having the ability to influence their behavior (emotions) and their actions so things can go in ones' favor or advantage."* David had a genuine desire to reconcile with Absalom. Yet, Absalom manipulated and use his father's affection and love to his advantage.

When Absalom appeared before David, he hypocritically humbled himself by bowing down with his face to the ground (2 Samuel 15:1-37). David kissed his son Absalom, showed him the greatest respect, full acceptance back into the family, and the king's grace. Yet, Absalom only had one motive for being with his father. He wanted the kingdom. When someone's motivation is contrary to the will of God, it is possible that they will eventually *lose their head!*

The Living Bible says that during battle, *"Absalom happened to meet the servants of David. Absalom was riding on his mule, and the mule went under the thick branches of a great oak, and **his head** caught fast in the oak, and he was suspended between heaven and earth, while the mule that was under him went on"* (2 Samuel 18:9). The head is a type or symbol of how one may possibly think. Absalom's only thoughts were to one day be king. He usurped authority and attempted to kill his own father! It was a deceptive mindset of manipulation that caused Absalom to literally *lose his head* (2 Samuel 18:14-15).

The Father's Kiss is God's grace, reconciliation and restoration. God is always looking down the road of life, waiting for a son or daughter to come back to His house. Although Absalom had come back to his father's house, the spirit of manipulation and ungodly ambition caused him to lose the *"new life"* his father David was positioned to provide. By the grace of God, Absalom had a chance for reconciliation and restoration. But Absalom rejected David's genuine love with an insincere "love" that was a fleshly imitation.

THE FATHER'S KISS

The Father's Kiss **Is Not** *A Fleshly Imitation*

A fleshly imitation pertains to that which is *"not genuine, it is counterfeit or carnal."* **The Father's Kiss** is always a genuine representation and manifestation of God's grace; holy in substance and nature (Luke 15:20). For the past several weeks, reports and allegations of sexual assault and harassment by celebrities and politicians have been in the news seemingly every day.

Tragically, there appears to be as much sexual misconduct in the church as there is amongst politicians and celebrities. Earlier we discussed Paul's admonishment to greet one another with a *"holy kiss"* in Romans chapter 16. However, the average Christian or church goer is not mature enough to greet someone with a *"holy kiss."* Notice what happens when our lives are not governed by the Lord.

The Bible tells us of Eli's sons, Hophni and Phineas who did not know or regard God. They acted wickedly—sleeping with women in the church (1 Samuel 2:22). It is hard to imagine these behaviors are occurring in the church today. Yet here are some recent newspaper headlines: *"Pastor in Tulsa, Oklahoma arrested for rape of a minor"* (who he forced to take "morning-after" pill after unprotected sex). *"Associate pastor charged with rape and sodomy of 13-year-old girl"* (more victims coming forward). *"Pastor charged with six counts of sexual crimes including molesting mentally-disabled woman in his care."* Fleshly imitation is that which is "not genuine, it is counterfeit or carnal."

We do not know the beginning or how these tragic sexual assaults occurred in any of the churches where these men served. It is heartbreaking to know these young women will have to live with the stigma of such violent acts for the rest of their lives. All we know is these church leaders succumbed to sins, transgressions and iniquities! As it was with Hophni and Phineas, so shall it be for those that engage in willful sins, transgressions and iniquities—judgment is coming!

The judgment of the Lord for Eli and his sons was *"Ichabod,"* the glory of the Lord was no more. Ichabod is a sign and symbol that the glory of God is departed and is no longer present (1 Samuel 4:21-22).

A fleshly imitation can begin with an innocent hug, embrace, or an inappropriate comment. The wise pastor, minister, deacon or member of the church must be prudent concerning contact and conversation with members of the opposite sex.

Additionally, the wise pastor or minister never meets with someone of the opposite sex alone, after hours, or after everyone else has left the office. This is a set up for disaster! 20 or 30 years of successful ministry can be destroyed with one allegation of indiscretion or immoral behavior towards a member of the opposite sex.

*"Remember them which have the rule over you, who have spoken unto you the word of God: whose faith follow, considering the end of **their conversation**"* (Hebrews 13:7, King James Version). According to the English Standard Version, it is written, *"Remember your leaders, those who spoke to you the word of God. Consider the outcome of their way of life and imitate their faith."* Both translations speak to the behavior and conduct of leaders in the house of God as *examples* and *ensamples* or ones who demonstrate by example.

Following the example and ensample of godly leaders as noted in Hebrews 13:7, we safeguard our hearts and govern our behavior in accordance with the integrity and character of God, where fleshly imitations have *"nothing in me"* (John 14:30 King James Version).

Although the Father's Kiss is both *natural* and *spiritual* in nature it is **NEVER** fleshy or an imitation. God *"kisses us,"* a sign and a symbol of His love and affection for us when He gives us examples of godly leaders to follow as models, mentors and motivators.

In The Voice Translation of 1 Corinthians 11:1, the Apostle Paul says, *"**Imitate me**, watch my ways, follow **my example**, just as I, too, always seek to **imitate the Anointed One**."* Paul's admonishment to the church is another means by which we can experience *The Father's Kiss*; just follow me, imitate me.

My entire family (children and grandchildren) have been made the better by *The Father's Kiss*, a sign and symbol of His love and grace through our pastors, Bishop Nate and Valerie Holcomb.

For almost 40 years of ministry, they have continually and persistently followed and imitated the Anointed One, the Lord Jesus Christ. By the way they live and lead, they express the grace and love of God for *"God is love"* (1 John 4:8 King James Version) by their actions and deeds. And to all of us at the Christian House of Prayer and Covenant Connections International, they say, follow me, imitate me; be an example of *The Father's Kiss!*

"You are a designer original. Do not allow negative imitations or the manipulation of others to keep you from your God-given destination."

Main Points: What The Father's Kiss Is *Not*

- The Father's Kiss is *not* entitlement. A basic definition of entitlement is, *"the belief that one is inherently deserving of privileges or special treatment."*

- The Father's Kiss is *not* manipulation. To manipulate someone is to *"have control over others by having the ability to influence their behavior (emotions) and their actions so things can go in ones favor or advantage."*
- The Father's Kiss is *not* a fleshly imitation. A fleshly imitation is that which is *"not genuine, it is a counterfeit or carnal."*
- God *"kisses us,"* a sign and a symbol of His love and affection for us when He gives us examples of godly leaders to follow as models, mentors and motivators.

Chapter 3: The Character of The Father's Kiss

*"Who being the brightness of his glory, and the **express image of his person**..."* (Hebrews 3:1a King James Version).

Character can be simply defined as the basic elements that makes a thing what it is. The essence, qualities, or traits that form the individual nature of a person or thing. More specifically, godly character is the moral compass that always points one back to the direction and attributes of God.

When Martin Luther King, Jr. said he looked forward to the day when all Americans would be judged solely *"by the content of their character,"* he was speaking of the traits which shape actions, conduct and behaviors of people.

The writer of Hebrews gives insight into the substance or nature, the essential qualities, and the attributes of the character of Christ. I do not believe that anyone can adequately describe or define all that He is; that is impossible. However, our discussion of the character of Christ is an effort to reveal key or central elements of God's virtue and moral excellence. In this chapter, we will discuss:

1. *The Image of Christ*
2. *The Substance of the Image*
3. *The Authority of the Ring*

The Image of Christ

In the King James Version of Hebrews 1:3a, the word *"express"* in the original Greek is *"character."* It means the *very stamp, mark,* and *impression*—the reproduction of God. To illustrate the *impression* or the *reproduction of God,* the writer utilizes the imagery and connotation of a king or governor and his signet ring.

If there was a document that a Roman emperor or governor wanted to send throughout his territory, he would take his signet ring, place it in hot wax, and stamp the document with the image of his ring.

With the image of the emperor's or governor's signet ring on the document, it became a representation of his authority throughout his territory—it was as if the emperor or governor himself was present.

According to W.E. Vines Expository Dictionary of Old and New Testament words, *"image"* is translated in this passage as *"eikon."* Eikon means *representation* and *manifestation*. The image of Christ is exhibited as a representation and manifestation of Jesus. This is the impression (*character*) in representation of the (*image*) that is the brightness of God's glory (Hebrews 3:1a).

Jesus Christ is the impression and image of God personified. The reproduction of God's character and nature; or that which makes Him who He is, and **The Father's Kiss** is a manifestation and reproduction of God's grace, reconciliation and restoration throughout His territory.

Psalm 24:1 says to us, *"the earth is the LORD'S, and the fulness thereof; the world, and they that dwell therein"* (King James Version). Jesus Christ is the impression and manifestation of God's grace. He is the substance of reconciliation and restoration given to the entire world (John 3:16)!

The Substance of the Image

Character can also be defined as the substance, essence, qualities, attributes or traits that form the individual nature of a person or thing. The substance of the image of God's character is love because God is love.

"Dear friends, let us practice loving each other, for love comes from God and those who are loving and kind show that they are the children of God, and that they are getting to know him better. But if a person isn't loving and kind, it shows that he doesn't know God—for God is love" (1 John 4:7-8 Living Bible).

The love of God compels the recipient of **The Father's Kiss** to serve because of God's great love. When you know you are loved, you are compelled to return that love through service. Therefore, the substance of the image of God's character (love) includes service.

The New Living Translation of Mark 10:43-45 says, *"whoever wants to be a leader among you must be your servant, and whoever wants to be first among you must be the slave of everyone else. For even the Son of Man came not to be served but to serve others and to give his life as a ransom for many."*

James and John had finished asking Jesus to grant them exalted positions of leadership in the Kingdom (Mark 10:37). Jesus's vision of leadership must have shocked his disciples because all they had ever known or seen before them was *positional* leadership. Many (including in the church) tend to seek position and power rather than opportunities for service or *servant* leadership.

After washing the disciples' feet, Jesus said, *"What I've done, you do. I'm only pointing out the obvious. A servant is not ranked above his master; an employee doesn't give orders to the employer. If you understand what I'm telling you, act like it—and live a blessed life"* (John 12:17 The Message Bible).

It is important to note when Jesus washed the disciples' feet, Judas was at the same table! Jesus knew it would not be long before Judas would betray him, yet He washed his feet anyway!

According to Luke 6:27-28, Jesus said, *"But I say to you who hear, love your enemies, do good to those who hate you, bless those who curse you, pray for those who abuse you"* (King James Version). Receiving and believing in the substance (love) of **The Father's Kiss** enables and empowers us to wash the feet of a person who may have betrayed us or mistreated us.

The substance of the image of God's character within our lives and leadership empowers and enables us to *do good to those who hate us, bless those who curse us, and pray for those who abuse us!* The King James Version of the Bible describes the character and image of God in Galatians chapter 5:22–23 by the attributes, traits or *"Fruit of the Spirit:"*

- Love
- Joy
- Peace
- Longsuffering
- Gentleness
- Goodness
- Faithfulness
- Meekness
- Temperance

As God's people, ***The Father's Kiss*** transfuses His grace in us through the Holy Spirit. We are given the *character* (the image) of Jesus; where we can freely love in joy and peace as He did. We can have patience along with kindness and faithfulness that can only come from the Father.

We can reflect the goodness of God while keeping our soul under control, operating under the Lord's control that empowers us to control self! For those who follow Him and live in and by the Spirit, these characteristics or fruits are a gift from God.

As we walk daily in the character and nature of God by the Holy Spirit, we become light in darkness (John 1:4-5) transforming the world, one life at a time by the light of Jesus Christ and the grace of ***The Father's Kiss***.

The Authority of the Ring

In the Living Bible Translation of Haggai 2:23, God says, *"I will take you, O Zerubbabel my servant, and honor you like a signet ring upon my finger; for I have specially chosen you,' says the Lord Almighty."* Haggai likens Zerubbabel to a signet ring that is a symbol of divine approval. The signet (ring) was also an emblem of ownership and authority.

It was used for the authentication of such things as royal directives or legal documents as discussed in the section of *The Image of Christ*. The signet ring provided the bearer or the one that wears the ring with the legal authority to act on behalf of the king. The signet ring portrayed Zerubbabel as one who represented divine authority and who appeared as the Lord's coregent.

Zerubbabel as the signet ring of God had the legal authority to represent the King of Kings! Representing the King of Heaven, Zerubbabel was given legal authority to restore the glory and majesty of the house of the Lord for the nation of Israel!

God established Zerubbabel's assignment and purpose. He said, *"The glory of this latter house shall be greater than of the former, says the LORD of hosts. And in this place, will I give peace, says the LORD of hosts"* (Haggai 2:9 King James Version).

THE FATHER'S KISS

The character of God had the ability to repair the broken-down walls of life's circumstances during the days of Zerubbabel. Just as God did then, He has done again! As God's signet ring, we have the legal right and authority as recipients and representatives of **The Father's Kiss,** to repair the broken-down walls of life circumstances and adversities that have sought *"to steal, and to kill, and to destroy..."*(John 10:10b King James Version).

Such was the dilemma of the prodigal. He had flipped the switch of *self-destruction* by his decisions that sought to steal, kill and destroy him. However, it was not too late! God is the God of *restoration* and *construction,* even from self-imposed acts of *destruction.* Although there had been hopelessness in the prodigal's mind and heart, his life and ministry were not over! As he received his *ring* and his *kiss,* from his father, he received *construction* and *restoration* for repairing the broken-down places of his life.

We have been granted this same legal authority as we receive and believe in the grace and empowerment of **The Father's Kiss.** When the Father gave the prodigal his ring and a kiss, it symbolized *reconstruction* and *restoration* of *authority.* Additionally, the ring and kiss were signs of the Father's embrace and grace of *acceptance, affirmation* and *reconciliation;* birthed from God's love, nature and character!

The father said, *"My son was dead, and is alive again; he was lost, and is found"* (Luke 15:24 King James Version). Just as the prodigal received new life, so is new life available for all that receive the embrace and grace of **The Father's Kiss**.

"Character cannot be developed in ease and quiet. Only through experience of trial and suffering can the soul be strengthened, vision cleared, ambition inspired, and success achieved." Helen Keller

Main Points: The Character of The Father's Kiss

- Character can be simply defined as the basic elements that makes a thing what it is.
- The image of Christ in Hebrews 1:3a, in the original Greek is *"charakter."* It means the *very stamp, mark,* and *impression*—the reproduction of God.
- The substance of the image of God's character is love, because God is love (Galatians 5:22-23 —1 John 4:7-8).
- The ring and the kiss is a sign and a symbol of the father's embrace of *acceptance, affirmation* and *reconciliation*.

- God is the God of *reconstruction* and *restoration* even from self-destruction.
- As God's signet ring, we have the legal right and authority as recipients and representatives of ***The Father's Kiss,*** to repair the broken-down walls of life's circumstances.

Chapter 4: You Have Not Many Fathers (Mothers)

*"For even if you had ten thousand others to teach you about Christ, you have only **one spiritual father**. For I became your father in Christ Jesus when I preached the Good News to you"* (1 Corinthians 4:15 New Living Translation).

When the Apostle Paul told the Corinthians *"You have only one spiritual father,"* he was reminding them of a bond and connection that he alone had with them. This bond was rooted in God's love for them; a love that would always be constant and remain the same. Tragically in America there are many that have never known this kind of love from their natural father.

According to an article written by Rosalind Sedacca, an estimated 24.7 million children live absent from their biological father. Almost 17 million children are living with their single mothers. Statistically, children who live absent from their biological fathers are more likely to be poor, and experience educational, emotional and psychological problems. Many times, these children are victims of child abuse and are more likely to engage in criminal behavior than their peers who live with their married, biological mothers and fathers.[3]

According to the Bible, God always wanted a family. Therefore, He creates the family (male and female) in His image after His likeness (Genesis 1:26.) He told them to be fruitful and multiply. God's message today is still the same, because He loves being our Father.

The primary word in the Old Testament for father is *Ab*. *Ab* designates primarily the term *begetter*, which carries the meaning of *bringing into existence*.[4] *Ab* also means, originator, chief, protector, or governor. The title of father is also used for one in authority.

When God created His family in His image and likeness He gave **them** (male and female) **dominion**, and the capacity to govern and guide. God empowered the female along with the male. A prolific Biblical example of female empowerment is found in Judges 4.

The New International Version of Judges 5:7 says, "*Villagers in Israel would not fight; they held back until I, Deborah arose,* **a mother** *in Israel.*" God took an ordinary woman with her gifts, strengths, and

---

[3] https://familyshare.com/21678/daddy-doesnt-live-here-anymore-how-absentee-fathers-are-affecting-our-kids. Accessed December 7, 2017.
[4] Strong, James. *Strong's Concordance*. Austin, TX: WORD*search*, 2007. WORD*search* CROSS e-book. Accessed March 10, 2018

weaknesses, and brought military victory through her unexpectedly strong hands.

The entire nation of Israel looked to Deborah as their leader.

> *"Now Deborah, a prophet, the wife of Lappidoth, was leading Israel at that time. ⁵ She held court under the Palm of Deborah between Ramahand Bethel in the hill country of Ephraim, and the Israelites went up to her to have their disputes decided. ⁶ She sent for Barak son of Abinoamfrom Kedesh in Naphtali and said to him, "The LORD, the God of Israel, commands you: 'Go, take with you ten thousand men of Naphtali and Zebulun and lead them up to Mount Tabor. ⁷ I will lead Sisera, the commander of Jabin's army, with his chariots and his troops to the Kishon River and give him into your hands. ⁸ Barak said to her, "If you go with me, I will go; but if you don't go with me, I won't go." ⁹ Certainly I will go with you," said Deborah. "But because of the course you are taking, the honor will not be yours, for the LORD will deliver Sisera into the hands of a woman"* (Judges 4:4-9 New International Version).

Deborah was a woman, and a wife called by God to be a judge and a prophetess. Her influence upon the people of Israel was so great and pervasive that she was called the *"mother of Israel."* When Deborah sent for Barak, the commander of the army, he was very straightforward, stating that he absolutely would not go into battle unless Deborah went with him! Barak did not have the faith to face the enemy alone. He needed to draw strength from the faith and strength of Deborah.

Deborah made it clear that she would go, but history would record the victory over their enemies came at the hands of a woman (Judges 5:15). Deborah's example indicates although we may not have many fathers, we also do not *have many (spiritual) mothers!*

As God's people not only do we need spiritual fathers, but we also need **spiritual mothers "created in His image and likeness"** (Genesis 1:26 King James Version). Solomon, the wisest man to ever live other than Jesus wrote, *"My son, listen to your father's instruction, and do not let go of* **your mother's teaching** (Proverbs 1:8 International Standard Version).

Proverbs 31 contains the influence, instructions, counsel and guidance of both a *spiritual* mother, that was also Lemuel's *biological* mother. The Bible shows us that everything Lemuel knew and understood about life and leadership, he learned and was inspired by his mother. *"The sayings of King Lemuel—an inspired utterance his mother taught him"* (Proverbs 31:1 New International Version).

"A few years ago, a greeting card company offered free cards to inmates at a prison to send for Mother's Day. Nearly all the prisoners took the offer and sent cards to their mothers. So, the greeting card company was encouraged by the success and they decided to make the same offer when Father's Day came around. They offered free cards for Father's Day, but they had zero takers. There was no one in that prison who wanted to send a card for Father's Day."

When I read the story above, I was reminded of Rosalind Sedacca's article that we referenced earlier. If the preceding story is true, it speaks to the influence of a mother and the tragic lack thereof of some fathers. Note the impact of a mother in the lives of 3 very influential men recorded in our history books:

> *"All I am I owe to my mother. I attribute all my success in life to the moral, intellectual and physical education I received from her."* **George Washington (1732-1799)**
>
> *"All that I am or ever hope to be, I owe to my angel mother."* **Abraham Lincoln (1809-1865)**

THE FATHER'S KISS

"You have omitted mention of the greatest of my teachers—my mother." **Winston Churchill**

The influence on world history of these 3 storied men is the direct result of the investment their mothers made in their lives; an investment for the betterment of their future. In 1 Corinthians 4:15, the Apostle Paul reminded the church of an investment for the betterment of their future that as their spiritual father he shared with them.

This same type of investment and influence is evident in the lives of women appointed and anointed by God to be *spiritual mothers* for the betterment of their sons and daughters.

The title of this chapter is "**You Have Not Many Fathers.**" What I submit to you is that we have not many fathers, but we also *do not have many mothers; and we need them both!*

We need *The Father's Kiss* of validation and affirmation; and we need *A Mother's Kiss* of validation and affirmation to steady and strengthen us. Every man, woman, boy and girl needs to know *The Father's* and *The Mother's Kiss* of grace; rooted in God's love. This is a love that is always constant and remains the same.

Main Points: You Have Not Many Fathers

- The Living Bible Translation of Judges 5:7 says, *"Israel's population dwindled, until Deborah became a mother to Israel."*
- Deborah's influence upon the people of Isreal was so great and pervasive that she was called the *"mother of Israel."*
- God shows we also need *spiritual mothers created in His image and likeness* (Genesis 1:26-27).
- We have not *many fathers*, but we also do not have *many mothers*; and we need them both.
- Proverbs 31 contains the influence, instructions, counsel and guidance of both a *spiritual* mother, that was also King Lemuel's *biological* mother.
- We need **The Father's Kiss** of validation and affirmation and we need **A Mother's Kiss** of validation and affirmation to steady and strengthen us.

Chapter 5: The Father's Kiss Validation Through Acceptance

*"To the praise of the glory of his grace, wherein he hath made us **accepted in the beloved**"* (Ephesians 1:6 King James Version).

The Pleasure and Purpose of the Father

When we look at the story of the prodigal, it is obvious that at some point he lost sight of the purpose and pleasure of the father for his life. The context of the parable in Luke 15 provides us with the fact that the father was wealthy.

The prodigal would one day inherit the wealth of the father, which is a part of the pleasure and purpose of the father simply because he is a son. However, what we also note in the prodigal's life is the apparent loss of his identity.

Proverbs 23:7 reminds us, *"...as he thinketh in his heart, so is he..."* (King James Version). At some juncture of his life, the prodigal's way of thinking began the process of the loss of his identity. Yet, he was not the only one that had this dilemma to arise in his life. The enemy's strategy concerning humanity has not changed since the beginning.

In Genesis 4:8-9, Cain had no respect for the purpose and pleasure of God's plan for his life. Cain had been robbed of his identity; an identity rooted in the fact that he was *"accepted in the beloved"* and he never knew that he had been robbed by the enemy!

When Cain's identity was stolen his reverence and respect for God was also stolen. Consequently, when Cain lost his respect for God, it is certain that he had no respect for his brother Abel! Now, since Cain had no respect for God or his brother, his disrespect led to murder (Genesis 4:8); all of which I attribute to the loss of his identity.

When a person loses their identity, which is rooted in God's divinity, the plots, ploys and plans of the enemy takes center stage of that person's life. We do not know for certain how Cain died. However, in Genesis 4:23-24, in The New Living Translation, we read these words:

> *"One day Lamech said to his wives, Adah and Zillah, hear my voice; listen to me, you wives of Lamech. I have killed a man who attacked me, a young man who wounded me. If someone who kills Cain is punished seven times, then*

the one who kills me will be punished seventy-seven times!"

According to some scholars and theologians, Lamech accidentally killed Cain while he was hunting with his son Tubal-Cain. In this theory, Lamech is a blind but skilled hunter, and his son Tubal-Cain accompanies him to direct his bow and arrow.

Hearing a noise in the bushes, they shoot what they think is a wild animal. Upon investigation, though, they discover that Lamech's arrow has killed Cain.[5] Had Cain not lost his identity in God's Divinity, Biblical history would have undoubtedly recorded his life story from a different perspective.

The 2017 identity fraud study released by Javelin Strategy & Research found that $16 billion was stolen from 15.4 million U.S. consumers in 2016, compared with $15.3 billion and 13.1 million victims a year earlier. In the past six years *identity thieves* have stolen over $107 billion.[6] The only sure plan to guard against identity theft as the people of God is to know that

---

[5] http://www.biblicalarchaeology.org/daily/biblical-topics/bible-interpretation/what-happened-to-cain-in-the-bible/. Accessed January 31, 2018.

[6] Internet Article: https://www.javelinstrategy.com/coverage-area/2017-identity-fraud. Accessed March 17, 2018.

we are accepted in the beloved and God has got us covered under the canopy of His protection.

God says to us in Psalm 91:1, *"He that **abides** in the secret place of the Most High shall abide under the shadow of the Almighty"* (King James Version). To abide is to live in, to dwell, to take up residence, to be covered. When we abide in the pleasure and purpose of the Father, we abide in the promise of Ephesians 1: 4-5. The English Standard Version of Ephesians 1:4-5 says, *"Even as he chose us in him before the foundation of the world, that we should be holy and blameless before him. In love he predestined us for adoption to himself as sons through Jesus Christ, according to the purpose of his will."*

The Voice Translation of this same passage says, *"God chose us to be in a relationship with Him even before He laid out plans for this world. He wanted us to live holy lives characterized by love, free from sin, and blameless before Him. He destined us to be adopted as His children through the covenant, Jesus the Anointed inaugurated in His sacrificial life. This was His pleasure and His will for us."*

From the foundation of the world, it was the Father's ***pleasure*** to ***choose us to use us because of the purpose of His will in Christ***. When God sent Samuel on a search to find the next king of Israel in 1st Samuel 16:7, He said of Eliab, *"Don't judge by his appearance or height, for I have rejected him. The* LORD *doesn't see things the way you see them. People judge by outward appearance, but the* Lord *looks at the **heart**"* (New International Version).

When God looks at the heart, He looks through and through, to determine genuineness of character. Although we may be flawed and imperfect, we are justified righteous because of Jesus' sacrifice (Luke 18:14).

The New Living Translation of 1 Peter 2:9 says, *"For you are a chosen people. You are royal priests, a holy nation, God's very own possession. As a result, you can show others the goodness of God, for he called you out of the darkness into his wonderful light."*

God chose us to be light in darkness from the foundation of the world! We are to illuminate the pathway to the Father's house, as well as reveal the endowment of God's grace, restoration and reconciliation. Knowing all the days of our lives that it is **The Father's Kiss** of His grace that protects and safeguards our identity in His divinity.

Adopted By The Father

When Paul speaks of being *"predestined for adoption"* in Ephesians 1:4, the word *"predestined"* means to, *"appoint before, to foreordain, to predetermine."*

The basic Greek word *"proorizo"* (predestined) means to *mark off or to set off* the boundaries of something. The boundary is marked and set off for the believer, and the set boundary is adoption as a child of God. According to Ephesians 1:5, *"He destined us to be **adopted** as His children through the covenant, Jesus the Anointed, inaugurated in His sacrificial life. This was **His pleasure** and His will for us"* (The Voice Translation).

From a natural perspective, adoption statistics are very limited. In the United States adoption became an official legal process (and not just an informal practice) in the 1850s. Over the past 150 years, this institution has evolved and changed along with society. Today, about **135,000** children are adopted in America every year — from the foster care system, private domestic agencies, family members, and other countries. Roughly 40% of adoptions are from the U.S. foster care system. There are currently 107,918 foster children eligible for and waiting to be adopted. The average age of a waiting child is 7.7 years old and 29% of them will spend at least three years in foster care.[7]

Focus On the Family provides a different perspective on adoption. Focus On the Family says

---

[7] Internet Article: http://www.goodhousekeeping.com/life/parenting/a35860/adoption-statistics/. Accessed January 8, 2018.

that currently, nearly **500,000** children and youth are in the United States foster care system. These children have all entered the system due to abuse, neglect or abandonment.

Of these kids in foster care, between 120,000 and 130,000 are considered legal orphans and are awaiting adoption into a permanent family.[8] Unfortunately, the foster care system will undoubtedly be with us always for a variety of reasons. Some parents cannot afford to care for their children, or some because of negligence or abuse have had their children taken from them.

The value of children in God's eyes is incalculable. We see this distinctive value of children in the Gospel of Luke. *"Then his disciples began arguing about which of them was the greatest. But Jesus knew their thoughts, so he brought a little child to his side. Then he said to them, "Anyone who welcomes a little child like this on my behalf welcomes me, and anyone who welcomes me also welcomes my Father who sent me. Whoever is the least among you is the greatest"* (Luke 9:46-48 New Living Translation).

The Equal Justice Initiative in Montgomery, Alabama states that many young children in America are imperiled by abuse, neglect, domestic

---

[8] Internet Article: http://www.focusonthefamily.com/parenting/adoptive-families/adopting-children/foster-care-adoption. Accessed January 8, 2018.

and community violence, and poverty. Without effective help and intervention, these children will continue to suffer, struggle, and fall into despair and hopelessness.

Some young teens cannot manage the emotional, social, and psychological challenges of adolescence and eventually engage in destructive, violent behavior that gets them arrested and charged as adults, although they may still be minors. [9]

We understand it is biologically impossible for a mother to be a father to a son. And, we further understand God may never lead us to adopt naturally one of the 500,000 children and youth in the United States foster care system. However, it is possible for us to *adopt a child spiritually* and care for them *naturally*. There may be a single mother with a son who needs a spiritual father in the church you attend or perhaps even in your place of work.

The Apostle Paul's message of hope and reconciliation expressed in **The Father's Kiss** is for the young man or young woman who had no other option but to become a part of the foster care system. The boundary is marked and set for that young man or woman to be adopted as a child of God

---

[9] Internet Article: https://eji.org/children-prison. Accessed January 8, 2018.

and transformed by the *renewing* of their mind to the mind of Christ (Romans 12:1-2, 1 Corinthians 2:16).

To be made just like Christ and conformed into His very image and likeness is the pathway to new and abundant life (Genesis 1:26, John 10:10). *"When someone becomes a Christian, he becomes a brand-new person inside. He is not the same anymore. A new life has begun!* (2 Corinthians 5:17 The Living Bible). There is new life in Jesus Christ!

A person is not able to rent a time machine and go back in time to start all over again. However, they can start right now and have a brand-new ending to their story! The same grace that saved us, is the same grace that can save that child that is in the foster care system.

When we take someone (a child, teen-ager or even an adult) into our lives and care for them, just as Jesus said-- *"Anyone who welcomes a little child like this on my behalf welcomes me, and anyone who welcomes me also welcomes my Father who sent me..."* (Luke 9:48 New Living Translation), we kiss God! This act of grace becomes a representation and expression of **The Father's Kiss,** validated by acceptance.

DR. GREGORY L. CRUELL

Validated and Accepted By the Father

Many of us as parents who have had children, recognized at some point that there may be one of our children that needed more attention than the other children. I have learned at this season of life, after 3 daughters and 9 grandchildren, that all of them are very different! Yet, even in their diverse personalities and approaches to life, I believe that as parents we would agree, ideally home should be a safe place, although for many, it was not.

The prodigal came to himself and recognized that his approach and attitude towards life was dysfunctional and he needed to get back to a safe place in life, which is the father's house and the father's love. When the prodigal got back to the father's house he was both *validated* and *accepted* by the father.

To be accepted is the heart cry undoubtedly of every man, woman, boy and girl; regardless of race, creed, color or religion. It is a search for significance. To be accepted simply means that *"I matter"* to somebody. When the prodigal came to himself; I submit to you, although he was in the "hog pen" of life, he understood he still mattered to his father.

I further submit that throughout our society and churches there is a silent request from many, *"Will somebody tell me I matter?* To verbalize a request of this nature is not easy because sometimes our struggles and troubles are self-imposed; as in the life of the prodigal.

Sometimes it is simply a person's behavior or conduct that is asking, *"will somebody tell me I matter?"* By riotous, unruly, disorderly living, the prodigal had lost sight of how much he mattered to his father. When he came to himself and went home, the prodigal experienced the *validation* of being *accepted* in the beloved despite his behavior and conduct that threatened to destroy his life.

There was a time in the history of Isreal that God said to His people, *"In your distress, (trouble) when all these things happen to you in days to come and* **you return to the LORD your God, then you will hear his voice.** *For God is compassionate. The LORD your God won't fail you"* (Deuteronomy 4:30-31 International Standard Version).

The prodigal's return to the father's house symbolizes a return to the ways of the Lord. The father's actions and compassion towards his son was the answer to the self-imposed struggles and troubles the prodigal had endured.

It was a reminder to the son, as God did with Isreal, *in your distress, when you return to the Lord your God, He will not fail you!* In other words, the son with unshakeable confidence knew that he mattered!

When Paul said you are "accepted in the beloved" (Ephesians 1:6), he was saying *in Christ, you do matter, you are significant.* Jesus died for our sins to *validate* His love for humanity. To validate means to *"prove that something is based on truth or fact."* Validation can also mean *"the recognition and acceptance of another person's thoughts, feelings, and behaviors."* What the prodigal discovered as truth was the fact that his father's love was grounded in *agape*—**unconditional love**.

Validation and acceptance builds relationships. One of the biggest problems in our society today is that we don't value one another. Subsequently, if we don't value one another we are certainly not going to trust or respect one another. Emotionally the son was broken and defeated. He felt like a failure and in his own words, *"I am no more worthy to be called your son"* (Luke 15:19 King James Version). However, the father *validated, accepted,* and restored his son as an heir and joint-heir!

The father's validation and acceptance created the bridge to reconciliation and restoration. The love of the father reestablished for the son that he mattered to the father, and the father wanted everybody to know and I'm having a party to honor my son! Validation and acceptance is a sign and symbol of the embrace and grace of ***The Father's Kiss;*** worthy of celebrating because we are accepted in the beloved!

Main Points: The Father's Kiss-- Validation Through Acceptance

- Ephesians 1:6b, *"He hath made us accepted in the beloved."*
- The enemy's strategy for humanity is to steal our identity.
- From the foundation of the world, it was and is the Father's pleasure to *choose us to use us because of the purpose of His will in Christ* (1 Peter 2:9).
- When Paul speaks of being *"predestined for adoption"* in Ephesians 1:4, the word *"predestined"* means to, *"appoint before, to foreordain, to predetermine."*
- Although God may never lead us to adopt naturally one of the 500,000 children and youth in the United States foster care system, it is possible for us to *adopt a child spiritually* and care for them.
- To validate means to *"prove that something is based on truth or fact."* Validation can also mean

"the recognition and acceptance of another person's thoughts, feelings, and behaviors."

- The prodigal experienced the *validation* of being *accepted* in the beloved despite his actions, behavior and conduct.
- Validation and acceptance is a sign and symbol of the embrace and grace of **The Father's Kiss;** worthy of a celebration!

Chapter 6: The Father's Kiss Validation Through Affirmation

"The moment Jesus came up out of the baptismal waters, the skies opened up and he saw God's Spirit—it looked like a dove—descending and landing on him. And along with the Spirit, a voice: "This is my Son, chosen and marked by my love, delight of my life." (Matthew 3:16-17 The Message Bible)

Affirmation is the Voice of the Father

The National Center for Fathering tells the story of a man alone on a date with his 6-year-old daughter. The aim of the date for the father was to make his daughter feel and know how special she is. At another point in the evening, an older couple walked by and placed a note on the table.

Here's what the note said: *"Sorry to spy, but my husband and I saw you out with your date and we were impressed with what a great father you are. From two adults that grew up without fathers, it is so important to have a solid male role model at a young age. Keep up the good work dad, dinner is on us!"*[10]

The King James Version of Matthew 3:17 says, *"And lo **a voice** from heaven, saying, this is my beloved Son, in whom I am well pleased."* The phrase "I am well pleased" in this passage means to *"think well of, to approve."* In its original Latin root, the word validate means to be *"strong, effective, or powerful."* It can also mean *"support of the truth or value of."*

Affirmation in its original etymology means *"to make steady or to strengthen."* Prior to fulfilling the purpose for which He was born, Jesus is affirmed by the voice of His Father in this passage. *"Then was Jesus led up of the Spirit into the wilderness to be tempted of the devil"* (Matthew 4:1 King James Version).

Knowing what was before His Son, what Jesus was about to endure, God ***affirms*** (*makes steady and strengthens*) and ***validates*** (*supports the truth and value of*) Jesus by saying this is my beloved Son in whom I am well pleased! The Message Bible translation of Matthew 3:17, God says, *"this is my Son, chosen and marked by my love, the delight of my life."*

Here is the point and central theme of this book. ***If Jesus as the Son of God was validated and affirmed in His life and ministry, how much more do we as***

---

[10] Internet Article: http://www.fathers.com/resource-center/. Accessed March 17, 2018.

THE FATHER'S KISS

God's people need the same! Some may need more affirmation than others, and others may not need much at all. However, if Jesus as the Son of God needed to be affirmed in life and ministry, so will you and me! Notable examples in the Bible include the fact that:

- God *validated* and *affirmed* the life and ministry of Enoch as he walked with God and was not because the Lord took him (Genesis 5:24).
- God *validated* and *affirmed* Moses when he asked God to take his life (Numbers 11:15).
- God *validated* and *affirmed* Joshua at Jericho when He appeared as the Captain of the Lord's Host (Joshua 5:13-15).
- God *validated* and *affirmed* Elijah when Jezebel threatened to kill him (1 Kings 19:1-4).
- God *validated* and *affirmed* Jesus because He was well pleased with Him (Matthew 3:17).
- Jesus *validates* and *affirms* the Centurion's faith by speaking the word of healing as his servant was sick and ready to die (Luke 7:7-9).
- Jesus *validates* and *affirms* Stephen by standing at the right hand of God as he is about to be stoned to death (Acts 7:55).

If these anointed and appointed servants of the Lord needed to be *validated* (*support of the truth or value of*) and *affirmed* (*steadied and strengthened*) it is crystal clear, so do you and me! The father that took his six-year-old daughter out on a date, recognized and realized that from a very early age, his daughter would need the strength of validation (*the truth and value of*) and affirmation (*to be steadied and strengthened*) from him as her father.

From the couple that paid for dinner that night, from their perspective this 6-year-old girl was *chosen and marked by love and was the delight of her father's life*. As a father of three daughters, I have learned that each one of them is unique and distinct and this was all by God's design. All three of my daughters are married now and I'm grateful, that every now and then they still need to hear my voice as their biological father.

God our *heavenly* Father has uniquely shaped and designed my daughters, as He has done with you and me, in accordance with His purpose for our lives.

God says to Jeremiah, *"for I know the plans I have for you, declares the Lord. Plans to prosper you, and not to harm you, plans to give you hope and a future"* (Jeremiah 29:11 New International Version). God knows full well what is in our future and therefore *validates* and *affirms* us for what He has prepared for us.

Acknowledging this fact, David says, *"You are my God." My times are in Your hand"* (Psalm 31:14-15 New International Version). When the father affirmed Jesus prior to going into the wilderness, Jesus knew that *His time,* represented by *His life,* was in the hands and will of His Father. As it was for Jesus then, so is it for you and me today! Our time, represented by the life that we live, is in the hands of the Father. *"Thy kingdom come. Thy will be done in earth, as it is in heaven* (Matthew 6:10 King James Version).

The voice of God the Father in Matthew chapter 3, steadied and strengthened Jesus as the Son to fulfill the purpose for which he had been birthed; to reconcile men back to God.

The Voice Translation of 2nd Corinthians 5:17-19 says,

> *"Therefore, if anyone is united with the Anointed One, that person is a new creation. The old life is gone—and see—a new life has begun! All of this is a gift from our Creator God, who has pursued us and brought us into a restored and healthy relationship with Him through the Anointed. And He has given us the same mission, the ministry of reconciliation, to bring others back to Him.*

It is central to our good news that God was in the Anointed making things right between Himself and the world. This means He does not hold their sins against them. But it also means He charges us to proclaim the message that heals and restores our broken relationships with God and each other."

The point of the story of the father that took his six-year-old daughter out on a date was to make his daughter feel and know how special she is. I would submit that the time that her father invested in her, both that night and future investments of time and understanding of how to succeed in life, helped to steady and strengthen her for her future.

Hearing the father's voice, both the voice of God, our heavenly Father and the voice of a biological or spiritual father sometimes the affirmation may simply be, *"You are enough. You don't have to be like anybody else because you are a designer original and as your father I love you for who you are."* This validating affirmation is an expression and manifestation of the **Father's Kiss.**

Affirmation is The Inspiration of the Holy Spirit

*"And **along with the Spirit**, a voice: "This is my Son, chosen and marked by my love, delight of my life"* (Matthew 3:17 The Message Bible).

To speak of *inspiration* in this context means to *infuse* or to be *filled* with the Spirit. The latter portion of Ephesians chapter 5:18 says..." *be filled with the Spirit"* (King James Version). *"Be filled"* with the Spirit is a command from the Lord which means that the believer is to be **constantly filled** with the Spirit; or keep on being filled.

The Spirit's filling is the personal manifestation of Christ in the life of the believer who walks obediently day by day (John 14:21). It is a consciousness of His presence and leadership—moment by moment or the **omnipresence** of the Holy Spirit.

The omnipresence of the Holy Spirit is seen in Psalm 139:7-8. David says, *"Where can I go from your Spirit? Where can I flee from your presence? If I go up to the heavens, you are there; if I make my bed in the depths, you are there"* (English Standard Version).

Then in 1 Corinthians 2:10-11, we see the characteristic of **omniscience** in the Holy Spirit. *"But God has revealed it to us by his Spirit. The Spirit searches all things, even the deep things of God. For who among men knows the thoughts of a man except the man's spirit within* *him? In the same way no one knows the thoughts of God except the Spirit of God* (King James Version).

In Matthew 3:16, the International Standard Version, the Bible says, *"When Jesus had been baptized, he immediately came up out of the water. Suddenly, the heavens opened up for him, and he saw the Spirit of God descending like a dove and coming to rest on him."*

In other words, the Holy Spirit had an active role in the affirmation of Jesus as He descended like a dove and rested on Him. 2 Timothy 3:16 says, *"All Scripture is **inspired** by God and is useful to teach us what is true and to make us realize what is wrong in our lives. It corrects us when we are wrong and teaches us to do what is right"* (New Living Translation).

The translation of the word *inspired* in the original Greek is *"theopneustos."* Theopneustos is a compound word comprised of *"Theos"* (God) and *"pneo"* (to breathe). Adam had no life in him until God breathed in him, the *"breath of life"* (Genesis 2:7). Whatever life a man or woman desires to live, there is no life accept it is *inspired* and given by God.

The prodigal eventually discovered that the life that he was living in the hog pen, was not an inspired life; the God kind of life. Living a life that is inspired, and God breathed, we discover and obtain the ability to make choices that the Lord has inspired or breathed for us in accordance with his will.

It was former First Lady Eleanor Roosevelt that once declared, *"I am today a result of the choices that I made yesterday."* Choice, not chance determines the life that I live and by the *inspiration* of the Holy Spirit, I choose the way of the Lord.

As God, the Holy Spirit, the third Person of the Trinity, as the breath of inspiration, He also functions as an agent of *affirmation*. As an agent of affirmation, the Holy Spirit by His presence also creates God breathed *aspirations*.

Affirmation Is Aspiration By the Holy Spirit

An aspiration is, *"a strong desire, a longing, aim or ambition."* Aspiration further defined is, *"a steadfast longing for a higher goal; an earnest desire for something above and beyond."* The ambitions and desires of the prodigal son had contaminated his sense of right and wrong.

When our *ambitions* are inspired by the Holy Spirit, our *aspirations*, will always be an earnest desire for something above and beyond what we want. The Bible reminds us, *"For as many as are **led** by the Spirit of God, they are the sons of God"* (Romans 8:14 King James Version).

The ambitions, desires and aspirations that the prodigal thought he *wanted* for his life is not what he *needed* for his life. When the Holy Spirit gives us an aspiration, a steadfast longing for something above and beyond, it is infused with the will of God.

God inspired aspirations carry the foundation of Joshua 1:8-9. *"Study this Book of Instruction continually. Meditate on it day and night so you will be sure to obey everything written in it. Only then will you prosper and succeed in all you do. This is my command—be strong and courageous! Do not be afraid or discouraged. For the* LORD *your God is with you wherever you go"* (New International Version).

Today, many people are placing their confidence and trust in the *motivation* of man, rather than the *inspiration* of the Spirit. Motivational speakers are filling auditoriums and venues to provide people with good *information* that many times is void of the *revelation* of God. I am not speaking negatively of motivational speakers, however the only problem with good is that good sometimes has one too many "o's."

In the New International Version of Joshua 1:8, God tells Joshua to *"study this book of instruction continually, only then will you prosper and succeed in all you do."* We have no indication that the prodigal considered God's way at any time in the decision to ask his father for a portion of his goods that one day he would eventually inherit (Luke 15:12).

The prodigal was not mature enough to handle overnight financial increase. Yet because the father loved his son, he gave his son what *belonged to him* as his father; the one that owned everything.

God provided Joshua with the blueprint and path for success in life and ministry that the prodigal disregarded from the pattern that he had seen in his father's house and in his father's life. There are many men that grow up without having a pattern or blueprint for life, let alone a pattern for success. Normally, when we talk about a successful person, our first thoughts are about someone with a lot of money.

But it is important to note that you can have a lot of money and still be unsuccessful in life! What this simply means is that it is possible to have success and not have *good success*. The prodigal's definition of success began with receiving his "portion of goods" or essentially a lot of money.

Wealth only provides options, not a guarantee of peace and contentment. Paul says to his son in the faith Timothy, *"godliness with contentment is great gain. For we brought nothing into the world, and we can take nothing out of it"* (1 Timothy 6:6-7 New International Version).

In The Modern English Version of Philippians 4:11, Paul says, *"I do not speak because I have need, for I have learned in whatever state I am to be content."* The original Greek word for content or contentment carries the meaning of *"being sufficient, or to be enough."*

The son had everything that he needed, in the father's house, but in his ambitions, goals and desires, it was not enough; it was insufficient. The richest people in the world are those that understand the value and riches of family. Family was so valuable to God, that he decided to create His family (Genesis 1:26-27). God's plan for creation was for men and women to marry and have children.

A man and a woman would form a *"one-flesh"* union through marriage (Genesis 2:24) and they with their children would be a family, the essential building block of human society.

The family is intended to be the place of God breathed *inspiration, affirmation* (make steady, and strengthen) and *aspirations* (an earnest desire for something above and beyond). The family is intended to be the place of God's grace and empowerment that is **The Father's Kiss**.

There is nothing wrong with healthy ambitions and aspirations. However, when our ambitions and aspirations become more focused on *money*, rather than *ministry* (servant leadership) to our family and community, it is possible that we will eventually find ourselves in the same place as the prodigal; in the "hog pen."

By example and ensample, Paul taught the church at Corinth to *"learn how to be content"* (Philippians 4:11 King James Version). As God told Joshua, as we study this book of instruction continually, (the Bible) only then will we prosper and succeed in *all* our God inspired aspirations (Joshua 1:8).

Affirmation Is The Validation of Sons Through Failure

Ernest Hemingway wrote a short story called" *The Capital of the World.*" Hemingway told the story of a father and his teenage son. The son had sinned against his father and in his shame, he ran away from home. The father searched all over Spain for him, but still he could not find the boy.

Finally, in the city of Madrid, in a last desperate attempt to find his son, the father placed an ad in the daily newspaper.

The ad read: ***"PACO MEET AT HOTEL MONTANA NOON TUESDAY ALL IS FORGIVEN PAPA."***

The father prayed that maybe the boy would see the ad and maybe - just maybe - he would come to the Hotel Montana on Tuesday at noon. When the father arrived at the Hotel Montana, he could not believe his eyes!

A squadron of police officers had been called out to keep order among the ***eight hundred young boys*** named *"Paco"* who had come to meet their father in front of the Hotel Montana! Eight hundred boys named Paco read the ad in the newspaper and *hoped* it was for them! Eight hundred *"Pacos"* came to receive the forgiveness they so desperately needed. All of whom needed to be validated as sons, receiving the approval of their fathers.[11]

In its original Latin root, the word validate means to be *"strong, effective, or powerful."* It can also mean *"support of the truth and value of."* Ernest Hemingway's story helps us to see the power of validation in a father's love.

The father in Hemingway's story attempted to reach and reconcile with his son. Yet, what the father discovered was the fact that there were ***799 other son's*** that desired to be reconciled to their fathers! The father was very purposeful in the ad that he

---

[11] Internet Article-https://www.crosswalk.com/family/parenting/dadswant-to-leave-a-legacy-affirm-your-children-11577399.html. Accessed January 10, 2018.

placed in the newspaper. He had searched all over the country of Spain and had been unsuccessful in locating his son.

What is needed in our society and I dare say even in our churches is a purposeful effort to locate and help *"Paco"* to come back home! *"Paco"* represents those men and women among us that have experienced some shape, form, or fashion of failure and have had no one to help them to be reconciled, restored and renewed.

It was the British Prime Minister, Winston Churchill that once said, *"success is never final, and failure is never fatal. It is courage that counts."* Failure, simply defined is a lack of success. Failure can also be the neglect of expected or required action by God. Micah 6:8 says, *"He has told you, O man, what is good; and what does the* LORD *require of you but to do justice, and to love kindness, and to walk humbly with your God"* (English Standard Version).

By not following the will of the ways of his father, the prodigal descended into failure. His father had raised him to be a man of justice or to do what's right. The prodigal's father had also taught his son what was good. The father had undoubtedly taught his son that authentic *humility* is always the key to abundant *prosperity* (1 Samuel 25:6, Psalm 35:27).

Ernest Hemingway's Paco lived in obscurity for a time in his life because like the prodigal, he did not follow or obey the ways of his father. Yet, it was the love of the father in Ernest Hemingway's story and the love of the father in Luke 15 that was the inspiration for persistently looking and searching for their sons.

Tragically, for many, *failure has become fatal.* It is vital that we understand that failure is only fatal when we maintain the mindset, actions and behaviors that *caused us to fail.* Failure is a *lesson* that can become a *blessing.*

Walt Disney was once fired by a newspaper editor because, *"He lacked imagination and had no good ideas."* Today, the Walt Disney Co. and its subsidiaries and affiliates are worth approximately $165 billion.[12]

Stephen Spielberg with movies like Saving Private Ryan, The Color Purple, Schindler's List and Amistad was rejected from the University of Southern California's School of Theater, Film, and Television three times.

Eventually, Mr. Spielberg attended school elsewhere, only to drop out to become a director. The unadjusted gross of all Spielberg-directed films exceeds $9 billion worldwide, making him the

---

[12] Internet Article: https://www.fool.com/investing/2016/09/08/how-much-is-the-walt-disney-company- worth.aspx. Accessed January 11, 2018.

highest-grossing director in history. His personal net worth is estimated to be more than $4.6 billion.[13]

Vera Wang. In 1968, Wang tried out and failed to make the cut for the U.S. Olympic figure-skating team. She later became an editor for *Vogue* magazine, only to be passed over for the editor-in-chief position.

Wang later began to design wedding dresses and now has a billion-dollar industry![14] For Walt Disney, Steven Spielberg, Vera Wang and countless other persons throughout life, they have learned that failure is a *lesson* that can become a *blessing*.

The story was once told of a newspaper reporter that approached Thomas Edison after he had created the lightbulb. The newspaper reporter said Mr. Edison how does it feel to finally be able to report that the lightbulb works? It has been said that you failed over 10,000 times! How does it feel to finally succeed? Mr. Edison replied to the newspaper reporter, young man, I did not fail 10,000 times; I simply learned 10,000 ways that it wouldn't work![15]

---

[13] Internet Article: https://www.forbes.com/sites/natalierobehmed/2016/12/14/from-george-lucas-to-oprah-and- jay-z-americas- richest-celebrities-2016/#4bc1a79e5959. Accessed January 11, 2018.

[14] Internet Article: http://www.wsj.com/articles/vera-wang-brian-grazer- and-more-on-failure 1427468012. Accessed April 26, 2015.

[15] Internet Article: https://www.forbes.com/sites/nathanfurr/2011/06/09/how-failure-taught-edison-to-repeatedly-innovate/#1f98b9cf65e9

The prodigal had failed, and Paco had failed, but the *failure* was not *fatal*, because they came back to their fathers; the place of blessings in abundance! The road back to the father's house means that to *move forward*, you must decide to *keep moving*.

What this further means is that as the people of God, assess *what* happened, *how* it happened, and *take* corrective measures to see that it does not happen again (even though it may); just **keep moving forward** in the grace of God!

Although as God's people, we may trip, we may stumble, and we may even fall, but when we get back to the Father, there is affirmation and validation in ***The Father's Kiss*** of grace and restoration. Proverbs 24:16 says, *"the godly may trip (fall) seven times, but they will get up again"* (New Living Translation).

Main Points: The Father's Kiss-- Validation Through Affirmation

- Affirmation in its original etymology means *"to make steady or to strengthen."*
- Eleanor Roosevelt once declared, *"I am today a result of the choices that I made yesterday."*

- Choice, not chance determines the life that I live and by the *inspiration* (God-breathed) of the Holy Spirit, I choose the way of the Lord.
- An aspiration is *a strong desire, a longing, aim or ambition. An earnest desire for something above and beyond.*
- The family is intended to be the place of God breathed *inspiration, affirmation* (make steady, and strengthen) and *aspirations.*
- Affirmation is the validation of sons even through failure.
- Failing does not make you a failure and when we get back to the Father's house, correction and instruction in righteousness is provided by the Father (2 Timothy 3:16).
- We may trip, we may stumble, and we may even fall, but when we get back to the Father, there is affirmation and validation in **The Father's Kiss** of grace and restoration.

Chapter 7: Why Every Son (Daughter) Needs a Father

> *"Guard your hearts. Be true shepherds over all the flock and feed them well. Remember, it was the Holy Spirit who appointed you to guard and oversee the churches that belong to Jesus, the Anointed One, which he purchased and established by his own blood. I know that after I leave, imposters who have no loyalty to the flock will come among you like savage wolves"* (Acts 20:28-29 The Passion Translation).

When a wolf has set its sight on a herd of deer, or elk, part of the strategy is to separate one from the rest of the herd and invoke fear. When fear or panic is awakened, a "flight or run response" is ignited within the herd. As the herd runs in panic, the wolfpack selects one among the herd to focus on.

Wolves do not run at full speed until they get as close to their prey as possible. At that point, they make a high-speed chase to test the animal. Wolves can keep this pace for hours on end and have been known to cover 60 miles in a single night. The real strength of a wolf is its endurance.[16]

In the Passion Translation of the Bible, in Acts 20, the Lord says to us, *"there are imposters who have no loyalty to the flock that **will come in like savage wolves**."*

Every son and daughter need protection, and direction established in the strength of correction and instruction by true shepherds, (fathers) because of the presence of *"savage wolves"* in the world in which we live.

Protection and Direction By Correction and Instruction

Consider the passage that began this chapter. The *guarding of one's heart* is critical in any relationship that is established or initiated. One of the most tragic Biblical examples of the presence of *"savage wolves"* was in King David's own family! David's lack of protection and direction, correction and the instruction of his sons Absalom and Amnon led to heartbreaking misery for his daughter Tamar in 2 Samuel chapter 13.

---

[16] Internet Article: http://www.wolfcountry.net/information/WolfObserved.html. Accessed January 13, 2018.

The tragic story of Amnon and Tamar is part of the disintegration of David's family after his sin with Bathsheba. Amnon was the half-brother of Tamar. Tamar is described as a virgin and beautiful, and Amnon was highly attracted to her (2 Samuel 13:1–2).

Amnon grabbed Tamar and tried to wrestle her into the bed. Tamar firmly refused the incestuous relationship, crying out, "No, my brother! . . . Don't do this wicked thing" (2 Samuel 13:12 New International Version). Amnon then forced himself upon Tamar and raped her (2 Samuel 13:14). Afterwards, Amnon was said to hate Tamar more than he had "loved" her before the rape occurred—it was never really "love" at all, but shameless lust!

It was not long before Absalom, Tamar's full-brother, found out about the crime committed against his sister by Amnon, and so did David. David's response was to become "furious" (2 Samuel 13:21 New International Version) but he took no real action. Absalom cared for Tamar in his own home and would not speak to Amnon. Two years later Absalom commanded his servants to murder his half-brother Amnon (2 Samuel 13:28–29).

We have no biblical evidence of David providing *protection* or *direction* for his daughter after she had been violently abused by a member of her family. In a place where she should have been safe, she was violated. Undoubtedly and tragically, Tamar lived with the abuse, rape, and incest, for the rest of her life.

According to the National Coalition Against Domestic Violence, in the United States, an average of 20 people are physically abused by intimate partners every minute. This equates to more than 10 million abuse victims annually.[17]

- Almost half of female (46.7%) and male (44.9%) victims of rape in the United States were raped by an acquaintance. Of these, 45.4% of female rape victims and 29% of male rape victims were raped by an intimate partner.
- 1 in 5 women and 1 in 7 men have been severely physically abused by an intimate partner.
- On a typical day, domestic violence hotlines nationwide receive approximately 20,800 calls.
- The presence of a gun in a domestic violence situation increases the risk of homicide by 500%.
- Intimate partner violence is most common among women between the ages of 18-24.
- Domestic victimization is correlated with a higher rate of depression and suicidal behavior.

---

[17] Internet Article: https://ncadv.org/statistics. Accessed January 15, 2018.

- 72% of all murder-suicides involve an intimate partner; 94% of the victims of these murder suicides are female.
- Between 2003 and 2008, 142 women were murdered in their workplace by their abusers.
- Nearly 1.5 million high school students in the United States are physically abused by dating partners every year.[18]

Domestic violence, rape and abuse in many of our homes continues to be a strategy of the enemy to destroy that which God loves; and that is the institution of family. Within the institution of the family is the incalculable value of mothers.

Mothers have a unique and crucial role in the lives of their sons and daughters. The love, care, nurture, and encouragement a mother gives is vital to the health and well-being of the family and cannot be replaced.

Yet, God created **man first** because men and (fathers) have the responsibility to provide godly leadership and well-being for their families. Every son, every daughter needs a father for protection and direction from predators both *natural* and *spiritual*.

---

[18] Ibid: Accessed January 15, 2018.

Paul reminds us in Ephesians 6:12, *"For our struggle is not against flesh and blood, but against the rulers, against the authorities, against the powers of this dark world and against the spiritual forces of evil in the heavenly realms"* (New International Version).

Domestic violence, rape, and abuse in any form is emboldened and led by *"spiritual forces of evil in the heavenly realm."* It is a father's responsibility to lead, to guide, and to protect sons and daughters from these spiritual forces, even when they don't believe or know that they need protection. Most of us, if not all of us as parents have had children that have either verbalized or thought that we did not understand them.

It is as if in their minds we've never been children or teenagers ourselves! Our desire as parents is to protect and direct our children and prepare them for life as responsible adults. Solomon advises parents to *"train a child in the way he should go, and when he is old he will not turn from it"* (Proverbs 22:6 King James Version).

Raising and training a child within the context of this proverb means it begins with the Bible, as *"all Scripture is God-breathed and is useful for teaching, rebuking, correcting and training..."* (2 Timothy 3:16 King James Version). Teaching our sons and daughter the truths of Scripture will make them wise for salvation

(2 Timothy 3:15) and thoroughly equip them to do good works (2 Timothy 3:17).

Teaching our sons and daughters enables them to give an answer to everyone who asks them the reason for their hope (1 Peter 3:15) and it requires discipline. Discipline is a vital element of correction and instruction for raising godly sons and daughter, for we know the *"LORD disciplines those He loves"* (Proverbs 3:12 New International Version). When you discipline your sons and daughters, you are teaching and training them the standards of virtuous behavior, that sometimes requires punishment and correction.

Thus, we should help our sons and daughters not take discipline lightly nor become disheartened by it as the Lord *"punishes everyone He accepts as a son"* (Hebrews 12:5-6 King James Version). Discipline, although it may seem unpleasant when received, will produce a *"harvest of righteousness and peace for those who have been trained by it"* (Hebrews 12:11 International Standard Version).

Teaching and training our sons and daughters in the ways of the Lord covers them under the canopy of God's protection, Psalm 91:

> *"He that dwelleth in the secret place of the Most High shall abide under the shadow of the Almighty. ² I will say of the LORD, He is*

my refuge and my fortress: my God; in him will I trust.³ Surely he shall deliver thee from the snare of the fowler, and from the noisome pestilence.⁴ He shall cover thee with his feathers, and under his wings shalt thou trust: his truth shall be thy shield and buckler.⁵ Thou shalt not be afraid for the terror by night; nor for the arrow that flieth by day;⁶ Nor for the pestilence that walketh in darkness; nor for the destruction that wasteth at noonday.⁷ A thousand shall fall at thy side, and ten thousand at thy right hand; but it shall not come nigh thee.⁸ Only with thine eyes shalt thou behold and see the reward of the wicked.⁹ Because thou hast made the Lord, *which is my refuge, even the most High, thy habitation. ¹⁰ There shall no evil befall thee, neither shall any plague come nigh thy dwelling. ¹¹ For he shall give his angels charge over thee, to keep thee in all thy ways.¹² They shall bear thee up in their hands, lest thou dash thy foot against a stone.¹³ Thou shalt tread upon the lion and adder: the young lion and the dragon shalt thou trample under feet.¹⁴ Because he hath set his love upon me, therefore will I deliver him: I will set him on high, because he hath known my name.¹⁵ He shall call upon me, and I will answer him: I will be with him in trouble; I will deliver him, and honor him.*[16] *With long life will I satisfy him, and shew him my salvation"* (King James Version).

Under the canopy of God's protection, we can trust the Lord to keep our sons and daughters from the negative and sometimes destructive influence of social media.

The Influence of Social Media On Our Sons and Daughters

In this age of social media and Internet access, the challenges of parenting are greater than they ever have been before.

Social media is a series of websites and applications designed to allow people to share content quickly, efficiently and in real-time. Most people today define social media as apps on their smartphone or tablet, which has transformed the way we function in modern-day society.

The Internet does have its *positives*, yet unfortunately we are faced all too often with its *negatives*. What we see many times specifically about the influence of social media is a mindset or a desire to be noticed.

The negative impact and influence of many social media user's centers on how many likes are acquired, received or how many people are following them on Facebook or Instagram, rather than any negative consequences that may follow.

An extreme and tragic example is Malachi Hemphill, 13, who accidentally killed himself while playing with a gun on Instagram while his friends watched him. The footage showed his mother and sister discovering him collapsed on the floor before they cut the feed.[19]

Although it may not be verbalized or thought of in this manner, underneath tragic deaths like Malachi Hemphill, sexual, revealing pictures by young men and women and personal information posted on Facebook, Instagram or some other means of social media, is the thought of, somebody notice me; somebody validate and affirm me!

In many regards, this type of mindset becomes silent, internal expressions or desires for somebody to notice me; born out of desperation to fit in or to be accepted and not rejected.

Nathan Dewall, a psychologist at the University of Kentucky says, *"For proof that rejection, exclusion, and*

---

[19] Internet Article: https://nypost.com/2017/04/12/teen-accidentally-kills-himself-on-Instagram-live-as-friends-watch/. Accessed January 18, 2018.

*acceptance are central to our lives, look no farther than the living room. "If you turn on the television set, and watch any reality TV program, most of them are about rejection and acceptance. The reason, DeWall says, is that **acceptance—in romantic relationships, from friends, even from strangers—is absolutely fundamental to humans.**"*[20]

In other words, somebody notice me; validate and affirm me. When the affirmation or validation does not occur, this is the place of assault on a person's mind. The Bible says that Satan is *"the mind blinder."* The New International Version of the Bible says, *"The god of this age has **blinded the minds** of unbelievers, so that they cannot see the light of the gospel that displays the glory of Christ, who is the image of God"* (2 Corinthians 4:4).

Satan as the mind blinder, *"god of this age"* (Internet age), is the major influence on the ideals, opinions, goals, hopes and views of everything that is contrary to the image of God, which is evil. Evil is live spelled backwards. All evil is the opposite of true life, the life of Christ (John 17:3, Romans 6:23).

When our sons and daughters are influenced by social media through the *"god of this age,"* rather than the influence of the Holy Spirit, they are led *away* from God, rather than *to* God. The acceptance and

---

[20] Internet Article: https://www.psychologicalscience.org/news/releases/social-acceptance-and-rejection-the-sweet- and-the-bitter.html. Accessed January 18, 2018.

inclusion they are seeking and searching for is in the truth that we are members of the family of God and loved by Him!

The New Living Translation of John 13: 34-35 says, *"Now I am giving you a new commandment: Love each other. Just as I have loved you, you should love each other. Your love for one another will prove to the world that you are my disciples."* God's love, our love for one another becomes a shelter from the influence of the god of this age.

The god of this age, the mind blinder also entraps many in what has been called a *search for significance*, without knowing their significance in Christ. The answer for significance is another way to say what has already been said; the importance of *validation through affirmation!* The influence of social media sometimes causes people to compare themselves to other people instead of fully recognizing that each one of us are Designer originals.

The English Standard Version of 2nd Corinthians 10: 12 says, *"Not that we dare to classify or compare ourselves with some of those who are commending themselves.* ***But when they measure themselves by one another and compare themselves with one another, they are without understanding."***

To the church at Ephesus, in the English Standard Version, the Apostle Paul says, ***"Put off your old*** *self, which belongs to your former manner of life and is corrupt through deceitful desires, and to be renewed in the spirit of your minds, and to put on the new self, created after the likeness of God in true righteousness and holiness"*(Ephesians 4:22-24 English Standard Version).

Paul recognized the influence of the former manner of life and its deceitful, destructive desires. Therefore, Paul encourages the church to be *"renewed in the spirit of your mind"* and come to the knowledge that your identity is in His Divinity!

To the church at Ephesus, as God reminds us today, we are Designer originals, created in His image and likeness (Genesis 1:26). There's no one like you anywhere in the world! God made you unique, distinct and on purpose, with a greater purpose in mind. As a Designer original, there is **NO ONE** that compares to the gift that God has created you to be to the world.

God has created you to be the light, life, and love that is so desperately needed in the lives of boys and girls, men and women around the globe. Jesus said in John 8:12, *"I am the light of the world. Whoever follows me will never walk in darkness but will have the light of life"* (King James Version).

As representatives of **The Father's Kiss,** we are called to be light in darkness! We are *"fearfully and wonderfully made"* (Psalm 139: 14 King James Version).

To know *who* you are and *Whose* you are, concretizes and solidifies the *significance factor* and the fact that I am a Designer original!

As representatives of **The Father's Kiss**, we have the responsibility to share God's grace with others that are still in dark, uncertain times or places of life. Providing light and hope in the fact that what God has done for me, He will do for you!

The root word of significance is *sign*. Since we are fearfully and wonderfully made in the image and likeness of God, we become a *sign* to those around us that guarantees *protection* of our mind.

The New International Version of Philippians 2:5 says, *"In your relationships with one another, have the same mindset as Christ Jesus."* In our relationships with our sons and daughters, members of our community and coworkers', protection and direction, correction and instruction are the *ways* of the Lord, found in the *word* of the Lord!

David at a very difficult time in his life (relationships with others) prayed a very brief prayer in Psalm 25:4-5. In this prayer David said, *"Show me your ways O Lord, guide me in your truth, and teach me"* (New International Version). Some have said that David was on the run from Absalom's rebellion and attempt to take over the kingdom. Others say that David was on the run from Saul, perhaps in the cave of Adullam.

What we do know for certain is that it was a very difficult time concerning key relationships in his life. When we don't know what to do, God will always show us what to do! When *savage wolves* appear (and they will), if our prayer is *show me your way O Lord, guide me in your truth and teach me*... God will do just that!

Choosing the way of the Lord guards our heart from this world's everyday gravity of negativity. Paul says to the church at Colossae, *"put on the new self, which is being renewed in knowledge after the image of its Creator"* (Colossians 3:10 English Standard Version). As a son or daughter of the living God, our assignment is to help others to choose to *put on* the Lord Jesus Christ. Just as we choose the clothes we wear every day, let us choose to *clothe ourselves daily* in the Lord!

As we put on the new self, renewed in the knowledge of our image in Christ, we insulate ourselves from the toxic assaults and attacks of *savage wolves* that can appear at anytime and anywhere. The efforts and attempts to destroy what God loves by the *god of this age* (Internet, social media) are rendered useless, inoperative and ineffective!

True shepherds (fathers) watch over sons and daughters. They are present to naturally and spiritually protect, direct, correct and instruct us. Investments in the lives of sons and daughters by fathers (shepherds) of this nature will never be forgotten.

It is these purposeful investments by fathers that are valued, trusted and respected that makes a difference in sons and in daughters that becomes *The Father's Kiss* of His grace, that will forever be embraced.

Main Points: Why Every Son (Daughter) Needs A Father

- Every son, every daughter needs protection, and direction established in the strength of correction and instruction by true shepherds (fathers) because of the presence of *"savage wolves"* in the world in which we live.
- David did not provide a place of *protection* for Tamar. Neither did David provide *direction* for Tamar after she had been raped by her brother Amnon and she lived with the abuse, rape, and incest, for the rest of her life.
- Discipline is a vital element of correction and instruction for raising godly sons and daughter, for we know that the "LORD disciplines those He loves" (Proverbs 3:12).

- When our sons and daughters are influenced by social media through the *"god of this age,"* the Internet age, rather than the influence of the Holy Spirit, they are led *away* from God, rather than *to* God.
- As a Designer's original, there is **NO ONE** that compares to the gift that God has created you to be to the world.
- When *savage wolves* appear, if our prayer is *show me your way O Lord, guide me in your truth and teach me...* God will do just that! (Psalm 25:4-5 New International Version)
- True fathers (shepherds) watch over sons and daughters. They are present to naturally and spiritually protect, direct, correct and instruct us.

Chapter 8: The Hope of the Father's Kiss

Throughout this book, the aim has been to communicate the grace of God's reconciliation and restoration that is in *The Father's Kiss*. In the preface, we discussed the reality of the crime perpetrated against humanity; and that is the fact that we all have been robbed of *The Father's Kiss.*

As we have heard and listened to the voice of God in this book, the question now becomes, what hope will our ministry sons and daughters, members of our churches inherit from us concerning the future of *The Father's Kiss?* As leaders, pastors, ministers, evangelists, prophets, and teachers are we imparting and endowing others with the grace of *The Father's Kiss?*

In historical terms, a legacy is something that is handed down from one period of time to another. Yet, the real strength of a legacy is about *learning* from the past, *living* in the present, and *building* for the future. Dr. Myles Munroe wrote *"we ought to go to the grave empty"* in his book ***Becoming a Leader.*** In other words, don't go back to heaven with the gift God gave us to give to others; specifically, **The Father's Kiss**; which is His grace.

When we speak of hope, we define hope as a confident, favorable expectation. In the Passion Translation of Hebrews 11:1, *"now faith brings our hopes into reality and becomes the foundation needed to acquire the things we long for. It is all the evidence required to prove what is still unseen."* The hope and the responsibility of **The Father's Kiss** is also carried in the spirit and command of Luke 12:48. *"Unto whom much is given, much is required"* (King James Version).

The Hope of The Father's Kiss

In Luke 7, the woman with the alabaster box illustrates the restoration of hope in the life of a woman who undoubtedly had lost hope. Luke describes her as a sinner; others describe her as a prostitute. Whatever her state or condition, she sensed a desperate need in her life.

The guilt and weight of her sin was more than she could bear. She ached for forgiveness and cleansing, for freedom and liberty. This woman approached Jesus despite all of her internal pain. She knew the public scorned and gossiped about her, and the so-called decent people wanted nothing to do with her.

THE FATHER'S KISS

At this point in her life nothing mattered to this woman except Jesus.

This was a *defining moment* for this woman. A defining moment is a time and place of transformation. It is a time and place that we will remember for the rest of our lives. It is the place where a certain decision is made, and we are transformed by that decision.

The devil had control of this woman's life. He had destroyed her self-worth and value. She had been used until she was almost used up and then **The Father's Kiss** of grace, reconciliation and restoration gave her hope for her future. Jesus said, "*Woman, thy faith hath saved thee; go in peace*" (Luke 7:50 King James Version). No matter who a person is, or where they come from, everyone has experienced some form of hardship or adversity and yet, even in the hardship or adversity, there is hope.

The story was told of a successful bank president by the name of Michael Downing. Mr. Downing was invited to speak to an auditorium full of wounded soldiers shortly after World War II. Soldiers that had experienced and endured life altering injuries and wounds were in the audience that day. These soldiers had endured shrapnel wounds, multiple gunshot wounds, amputations, loss of limbs, horrific burns and mind-altering battlefield trauma. They would live with the effects of their injuries for the rest of their lives.

As Mr. Downing stood before this auditorium full of wounded soldiers, he began his speech by saying, *"I want you to know, that you have a bright future. Anything is possible, and you have the potential to achieve anything that you desire."* Almost immediately, several soldiers started to boo Mr. Downing. One soldier stood to his feet and said, "Look around this room, how dare you speak to us in this manner. Are you blind!?"

Mr. Downing had been standing at a podium in the center of the stage, but after those remarks from the soldier, Mr. Downing slowly sat in a nearby chair.

As Mr. Downing sat, he slowly removed his prosthetic right leg. He then removed his prosthetic left leg, left arm and left hand. Then, Mr. Downing sitting there a stump of a man, began his speech all over again. *"I want you to know, that you have a bright future. Anything is possible, and you have the potential to achieve anything that you desire!"*

What the soldiers did not know is that as a little boy, Mr. Downing had fallen off the back of his father's wagon into subzero weather during a snowstorm. His body was exposed for over 14 hours, and the amputations were necessary to save his life.

What Mr. Downing did for that auditorium of wounded soldiers, is what **The Father's Kiss** does for all that have been wounded on the battlefields of life. Mr. Downing restored hope, where hope had

THE FATHER'S KISS

been lost. Although the physical, natural wounds remained with the soldiers, *spiritual* seeds of hope, healing and peace were planted in their lives.

The woman with the alabaster box received ***The Father's Kiss*** of grace, reconciliation, restoration, validation and affirmation when Jesus said, *"Woman thy faith has saved thee, go in peace."* Jesus provided hope and healing for her future. Faith in the grace of God has more healing ability than all the pharmacies in the world. Faith in the grace of God restores hope where hope has been lost.

According to Romans 4:16-22:

> *"16 Therefore, the promise comes by faith, so that it may be by grace and may be guaranteed to all Abraham's offspring—not only to those who are of the law but also to those who have the faith of Abraham. He is the father of us all. 17 As it is written: I have made you a father of many nations. He is our father in the sight of God, in whom he believed—the God who gives life to the dead and calls into being things that were not. 18 Against all hope, Abraham in hope believed and so became the father of many nations, just as it had been said to him, so shall your offspring be. 19 Without weakening in his faith, he faced the fact that his body*

> *was as good as dead—since he was about a hundred years old—and that Sarah's womb was also dead.* [20] **Yet he did not waver through unbelief regarding the promise of God but was strengthened in his faith and gave glory to God.** [21] *Being fully persuaded that God had power to do what he had promised.* [22] *This is why it was credited to him as righteousness."* (New International Version)

God made Abraham a promise that he stood upon. Abraham hoped against hope. It seemed as if nothing else could be done, yet Abraham **chose to have faith in God.**

"If you only have faith in God—this is the absolute truth—you can say to this Mount of Olives, 'Rise up and fall into the Mediterranean,' and your command will be obeyed. All that's required is that you really believe and have no doubt! Listen to me! **You can pray for anything, and if you believe, you have it; it's yours**" (Mark 11:22-24 The Living Bible).

It does not matter what battles of life we may have endured. It does not matter what our individual sins, transgressions or iniquities may have been in the past or maybe in the present; have faith in God! He is the restorer of lost hope. You may have endured the reality of a divorce, bankruptcy, incarceration of a son, daughter or husband, or foreclosure on your home; know *"His grace is sufficient for you"* (2 Corinthians 12:7 King James Version).

Validated and affirmed by her faith in God, the woman with the alabaster box was taken from sorrow to the restoration of hope for the future. This woman realized that she had been made brand new by God's grace, restoration and reconciliation and what Jesus said to her, He says to us, *"now go in peace"* (Luke 7:50 King James Version), your future is bright.

Main Points: The Hope of The Father's Kiss

- What God gave to us, He intended for us to give to others; specifically, **The Father's Kiss**.
- A defining moment is a time and place of transformation.
- The woman with the alabaster box received The Father's Kiss of grace, power of reconciliation and the strength of restoration when Jesus said, *"Woman thy faith has saved thee, go in peace."* The Father's Kiss of grace provided hope and healing for her future (Luke 7:50).
- Abraham in hope believed and so became the father of many nations (Romans 4:18 New International Version).

- You may have endured the reality of a divorce, incarceration of a son, daughter or husband, foreclosure on your home, just know by **The Father's Kiss**, *"His grace is sufficient for you"* (2 Corinthians 12:7 King James Version).
- God wants you to know, that you have a bright future. Anything is possible, and you have the potential to achieve anything that you desire!

Chapter 9: The Legacy of The Father's Kiss

Learning From the Past, Living In the Present, Building For the Future

An authentic legacy is about life and living. It's about *learning* from the past, *living* in the present, and *building* for the future. In Genesis 38:1-30, we witness character traits in the life of Judah that are not *praiseworthy*, even though Judah's name means *praise*. By no means do I sit in judgment of Judah, because *"all have sinned* (including yours truly) *and have come short of the glory of God"* (Romans 3:23 King James Version).

Yet Judah's legacy helps us learn from the past, enables us to live in the present, and permits us to build for our future. The Bible tells us that Judah had two sons, Er and Onan. They were wicked men and died early. In those days, it was customary for the eldest son to marry first. If he died before his wife had a son, the next brother had to marry his widow and raise offspring for him. Well, Judah's first and second son married Tamar.

Neither of them produced children with her. So, Judah viewed Tamar as a cursed woman. Although he had one more son, he was reluctant to have his youngest son to marry her.

Judah told Tamar to wait for Shelah to reach manhood. However, after Shelah had become a man, Judah did not permit him to marry her (Genesis 38:6-14). In the process of time, Judah's wife died. After he had mourned for his wife, he headed to a place called Timnath to shear his sheep.

Upon hearing this news of her father-in-law's travels, Tamar disguised herself as a prostitute. She immediately went to Enaim which was in route to Judah's destination. Upon arriving at Enaim, he saw a woman but did not recognize her because of the veil worn over her face.

Thinking she was a prostitute, he requested her services. Tamar's plan was to become pregnant by this ruse so she might bear a child in Judah's line. Since Judah had not given her to Shelah, she played the part of a prostitute! Tamar struck a bargain with Judah for the prize of a goat, secured by his staff, seal, and cord.

Later, Judah sent a goat to Enaim to exchange for his staff, seal, and cord. The woman was nowhere to be found. No one knew of any prostitute in Enaim

(Genesis 38:12-23) and three months later, Tamar was accused of prostitution because of her pregnancy.

Upon hearing this news, Judah ordered that she be burned to death. Tamar sent the staff, seal, and cord to him with a message declaring that the owner of these items was the man who had made her pregnant. Upon recognizing these items as his own, Judah released Tamar from her death sentence.

The narrative in Genesis makes a note that Judah did not have further sexual relations with Tamar (Genesis 38:24-30). Thus, Tamar secured her place in the family as well as Judah's posterity. She gave birth to twins, Perez and Zerah. Perez is later identified in the Book of Ruth as the ancestor of King David (Ruth 4:18-22). According to the Gospel of Matthew, Judah and Tamar are ancestors of Jesus through their son Perez (Matthew 1:1-3).

Despite the sinful events of Genesis 38, Judah was not removed as a progenitor of the Messianic line. The line of the Messiah did not come through Joseph, as we might expect -- it came through Judah and Tamar. God **did not condone** their wrongdoing, but this fact clearly demonstrates His amazing grace! What we *learn* from the past, to *live* in the present, to *build* for the future is the fact that **God's grace, The Father's Kiss, works even in the dirt!**

Dirt can be defined, *"as mud or dust, that which soils or makes unclean someone or something. Any unclean matter that soils; that which is filthy, or contemptible; or birthed of corruption."* To heal a man born blind, Jesus *"spat on the ground, made some mud with the saliva, and put it on the man's eyes"* (John 9:6, English Standard Version).

The grace of God, as seen in Jesus, the Son of God, ***works even in the dirt.*** Jesus used spit and dirt as a sign of His grace (*the power and equipment for ministry*) and healed a man; blind from his birth. Even though Judah was corrupted, soiled and fell into sexual immorality with his daughter-in-law Tamar, God worked in the *"dirt"* of his life. History will forever record that ***Jesus is the Lion of the tribe of Judah*** (Revelation 5:5) ***and called the son of David!***

There was a time in the life of King David, a member of Jesus lineage, where he also could be considered to have been a *blind man*. God had given David everything that he wanted, everything that he needed, and had made him king of all Israel, but he was blinded by the sin of lust! To the extent David had a man that was his friend and loyal servant, put on the front lines of the battle, to be killed in order that he could have his friend's wife for his own (2 Samuel 11). When Nathan the prophet came and revealed David's sin, transgression and iniquity, David responded to the *"dirt"* in his life by writing Psalms 51.

THE FATHER'S KISS

Specifically, in verse 17 David penned, *"The sacrifice you desire is a broken spirit. You will not reject a broken and repentant heart, O God"* (New Living Translation). To repent is to turn away from sin and turn to God. David had been blinded by the dirt of his own lust for Bathsheba. He could not see his *sin* that was upward toward God, his *transgression* against Uriah and the *iniquity* that was bent and twisted inside him.

What we learn from David's past, to live in the present, and to build for the future is the endowment of **The Father's Kiss** despite our *dirt* and wrong doings. God called David a man after his own heart because David was *obedient* and *repentant*. When confronted with the sin of adultery and the murder of Bathsheba's husband, David was *obedient* to the correction of God through Nathan and quickly accepted responsibility and *repented* (2 Samuel 12:7).

In response to Nathan revealing what David thought was *secret sin*, David wrote in Psalm 51: 1-2, *"Look on me with a heart of mercy, O God, according to Your generous love. According to Your great compassion, wipe out every consequence of my shameful crimes. Thoroughly wash me, inside and out, of all my crooked deeds. Cleanse me from my sins!"* (The Voice Translation)

We learn 4 lessons from David's past, to live in the present, and to build our future. *First*, secret sin will be uncovered. *Second*, God will forgive anyone who repents. *Third*, sin's consequences remain even when the sin is forgiven. And *fourth*, **God's grace still works in our dirt!** Although the first child born to David and Bathsheba died, their next son, Solomon, became heir to the throne (1 Kings 1:32-35).

Even in our dirt, God always has a plan for man. When Adam and Eve were soiled and corrupted, made dirty by disobedience in the Garden of Eden, the strategy of the enemy was the destruction of humanity. Yet, God always had a plan for man.

To Jeremiah God said, *"For I know the plans I have for you. Plans to prosper you and not harm you. Plans to give you hope and a future"* (Jeremiah 29:11 New International Version). God further spoke to Jeremiah in the New International Version of chapter 24:7, *"I will give them a heart to know that I am the LORD, and they shall be my people and I will be their God, for they shall return to me with their whole heart."*

Our sinful hearts undergo surgery by the hand of the Lord and He gives us *"a heart to know the Lord."* A heart filled with compassion, forgiveness, kindness, grace and hope because God *"knows the plans that He has for us."* It is God's will, that you and me are engrafted into His legacy!

As was discussed earlier, a legacy is about *learning* from the past, *living* in the present, and *building* for the future. Jesus establishes a very clear and concise example of legacy with his disciples in John 13:14-17.

> *"And since I, your Lord and Teacher, have washed your feet, you ought to wash each other's feet. [15] I have given you an example to follow. Do as I have done to you. [16] I tell you the truth, slaves are not greater than their master. Nor is the messenger more important than the one who sends the message. [17] Now that you know these things, God will bless you for doing them"* (New Living Translation).

When Jesus washed the disciples' feet, it is important to note Judas was also at the table. Jesus knew full well that Judas was going to betray him, yet He washed his feet! A portion of the legacy Jesus wanted to leave for His disciples was the fact that we should do ***everything from the heart of a servant.***

The Bible never provides any evidence of Judas having the heart of a servant as personified by Jesus. While we cannot be certain as to the reason why Judas betrayed Jesus, some things are clear.

Although Judas was chosen to be one of the twelve, all scriptural evidence points to the fact that he ***never believed Jesus to be God*** (John 6:64). Judas not only lacked faith in Christ, but he had little or no personal relationship with Jesus.

When the synoptic gospels list the twelve, they are always listed in the same general order with slight variations (Matthew 10:2-4; Mark 3:16-19; Luke 6:14-16). The general order is believed to indicate the relative closeness of their personal relationships with Jesus.

Despite the variations, Peter, James and John are always listed first. This is consistent with their relationships with Jesus. Judas is always listed last, which may indicate his relative lack of a personal relationship with Christ. The latter portion of Matthew 27:5 states, *"And he went and hanged himself"* (King James Version). Jesus love for Judas never changed, but without a saving relationship through Christ, *Judas eventually hung himself!*

A legacy, *learning* from the past, *living* in the present, and *building* for the future includes **washing everybody's feet**; which may sometimes include our own personal Judas. Don't worry about your Judas, if his or her heart is not right, they will eventually hang themselves!

When our sins, transgressions, and iniquities *"made us dirty,"* when we came to ourselves, and came back to the Father, the Father *"kissed us"* with His grace. God's grace, brought *reconciliation, restoration, validation* and *affirmation* that began a *celebration* in the Father's house (Luke 15:23)!

Just as it was with Adam and Eve; Judah and Tamar; King David and the prodigal, God's grace is sufficient (2 Corinthians 12:9). When a man or woman turns from their sin, we come face to face with God's grace!

The prodigal said, *"Father, I have sinned against heaven, and in thy sight, and I am no more worthy to be called thy son"* (Luke 15:21 King James Version). The Father wasn't concerned about the sins of his son. The son's repentance replaced *disgrace* with the unmerited *grace* of the Father!

The father ordered the servants to bring the best robe. No doubt it was one of his own—a sign of dignity and honor, proof of the prodigal's acceptance back into the family! There was a ring placed upon the son's hand, a sign of authority and sonship, and sandals were placed on his feet.

Every item represented the gift of salvation. The robe of the *Redeemer's righteousness* (Isaiah 61:10), the privilege of partaking of the *Spirit of adoption* (Ephesians 1:5), and feet fitted with the readiness that comes from the *gospel of peace*, prepared to *walk in the ways of holiness* (Ephesians 6:15)!

The New Living Translation of Luke 15:20 states, "And while he (the son) was still a long way off, his father *saw him coming. Filled with love and compassion, he ran to his son, embraced him, and **kissed him**."* The father's focus was not on what His son had done. The father's focus was, *"This son of mine was dead and has now returned to life. He was lost, but now he is found. Let the party begin!"* (Luke 15:24-New Living Translation)

This was not just any party; it was a rare and complete celebration. Had the boy been dealt with according to the Law, there would have been a funeral, not a celebration! What the prodigal had lost, by *grace*, *reconciliation* and *restoration* was now his again by **The Father's Kiss**.

The word reconcile in the original Greek means, *"to change, or exchange."* Hence, *"To change from enmity to friendship, to exchange wrong for right."* Regarding the relationship between God and man, reconciliation is what God accomplishes by exercising His saving grace towards us (Ephesians 2:8).

To restore literally means to *"give back"* that which existed before. The emphasis for us as the people of God is *separation* from the former, negative influences of the world to a giving back, a *restoration* of God's original plan for man. God's original plan for man has always been for us *"to have dominion"* and not be *"dominated"* (Genesis 1:26).

Receiving **The Father's Kiss**, the embrace of God's grace, reconciliation and restoration frees us from being dominated by our past. Receiving the Father's Kiss engrafts us into the legacy of Christ, *living* in the present, and *building* for the future. This ultimately and finally heals us and makes us whole, *"spirit, soul and body"* (1 Thessalonians 5:23). *"If the Son sets you free, you will indeed be free"* (John 8:36 Living Bible). We have been set free from our past sins, transgressions and iniquities by **The Father's Kiss** of grace, restoration, reconciliation and affirmation. Child of God, celebrate, dance like nobody is watching! It's time to let your party begin!

Main Points: The Legacy of The Father's Kiss

- All have sinned and have come short of the glory of God (Romans 3:23 King James Version).
- God's grace, The Father's Kiss, works in the dirt!
- Dirt can be defined, "as that which makes unclean someone or something. Any unclean matter that soils, that which is filthy, or contemptible; or birthed of corruption."
- A legacy—*learning* from the past, *living* in the present, and *building* for the future includes **washing everybody's feet**; which may sometimes include your own personal Judas.

- Regarding the relationship between God and man, reconciliation is what God accomplishes by exercising His grace towards us—His unmerited favor (Ephesians 2:8).
- Receiving **The Father's Kiss**, the embrace of God's grace, reconciliation and restoration frees us from being dominated by past.
- Receiving the Father's Kiss engrafts us into the legacy of Christ, *living* in the present, and *building* for the future.
- Child of God, celebrate, dance like nobody is watching! Let your party begin!

Epilogue

Years ago, there was a very wealthy man who, with his devoted young son, shared a passion for art collecting. Together they traveled around the world, adding only the finest art treasures to their collection. Priceless works by Picasso, Van Gogh, Monet and many others adorned the walls of the family estate. The widowed elder man looked on with satisfaction as his only child became an experienced art collector. The son's trained eye and sharp business mind caused his father to beam with pride as they dealt with art collectors from around the world.

As winter approached, war engulfed the nation, and the young man left to serve his country. After only a few short weeks, his father received a telegram. His beloved son was missing in action. The art collector anxiously awaited more news, fearing he would never see his son again.

Within days, his fears were confirmed; the young man was killed while rushing a fellow soldier to a medic. Distraught and lonely, the old man faced the upcoming Christmas holidays with anguish and sadness. The joy of the season, that he and his son had so looked forward to, would visit his house no longer. On Christmas morning, a knock on the door awakened the depressed old man.

As he walked to the door, the masterpieces of art on the walls only reminded him that his son was not coming home. As he opened the door, he was greeted by a soldier with a large package in his hands.

He introduced himself to the man by saying, "I was a friend of your son's. I was the one he was rescuing when he was killed. May I come in for a few moments? I have something to show you." As the two began to talk, the soldier told of how the man's son had told everyone of his, not to mention his father's, love of fine art.

"I am an artist," said the soldier, "and I want to give you this." As the old man unwrapped the package, the paper gave way to reveal a portrait of the man's son. Though the world would never consider it the work of a genius, the painting featured the young man's face in striking detail.

Overcome with emotion, the man thanked the soldier, promising to hang the picture above the fireplace. A few hours later, after the soldier had departed, the old man set about his task. True to his word, the painting went above the fireplace, pushing aside thousands of dollars' worth of the finest collection of art treasures. His task completed, the old man sat in his chair and spent Christmas gazing at the gift he had been given.

During the days and weeks that followed, the man realized that even though his son was no longer with him, the boy's life would live on because of those he had touched. He would soon learn that his son had rescued dozens of wounded soldiers before a bullet stilled his caring heart.

As the stories of his son's gallantry continued to reach him, fatherly pride and satisfaction began to ease his grief. The painting of his son soon became his most prized possession, far eclipsing any interest in the pieces for which museums around the world clamored. He told his neighbors it was the greatest gift he had ever received.

The following spring, the old man became ill and passed away. The art world was in anticipation of the priceless treasures that would be sold at auction with the collectors passing. According to the will of the old man, all of the art works would be auctioned on Christmas Day, the day he had received his greatest gift. The day soon arrived and art collectors from around the world gathered to bid on some of the world's most spectacular paintings. Dreams would be fulfilled this day; greatness would be achieved as many would claim, "I have the greatest art collection in the world."

The auction began with a painting that was not on any museum's list. It was the painting of the man's son. The auctioneer asked for an opening bid, but the room was silent. "Who will open the bidding with $100?" he asked. Minutes passed, and no one spoke. From the back of the room came a voice, "Who cares about that painting? It's just a picture of his son." "Let's forget about it and move on to the good stuff," more voices echoed in agreement. "No, we must sell this one first," replied the auctioneer.

"Now, who will take the son?" Not one person budged, until finally, a neighbor of the old man spoke, "Will you take $10.00 for the painting? That's all I have.

I knew the boy, so I'd like to have it." "I have ten dollars. Will anyone go higher?" called the auctioneer. After more silence from the disgruntled audience, the auctioneer said, "Going once, going twice, gone." The gavel fell. Cheers filled the room, and someone exclaimed, "Now we can get on with it and bid on the real treasures!"

Then, the auctioneer looked at the audience and announced that the auction was over! Stunned disbelief quieted the room. Someone spoke up and asked, "What do you mean, it's over? We didn't come here for a picture of some old guy's son. What about all the paintings? There are millions of dollars' worth of art here! I demand that you explain what is going on!" The auctioneer replied, *"It's very simple. According to the will of the father, whoever gets the son ... gets it all."*

Unknown

This is the message of **The Father's Kiss**. According to the will of the Father whoever gets Jesus as the Son, **gets it all! The Father's Kiss** reveals God's grace, reconciliation, restoration and validation through affirmation. When we receive Jesus, we get it all!

This is where as a *"holy nation"* (1 Peter 2:9 English Standard Version) of God's people we are authorized to bestow and share **The Father's Kiss** of grace, of reconciliation and restoration by the ***character of God's love*** (Galatians 5:22-23). It is in the character of God's love that a *"holy kiss "*is expressed. Which has nothing to do with one's *sexuality* but everything to do with the *reality* of the love of God for us all (John 3:16).

It was the sovereignty of God that carried me to a barber shop in Junction City Kansas in the spring of 2003. The sovereignty of God also brought a father and son to the same barber shop that morning where I was waiting to get a haircut. It was no accident or coincidence. It was the providence and sovereignty of God that brought us together that day for me to witness and receive a message of God's love for us all.

There has been a time in all our lives where we had lived the life of the prodigal son. But this book has not been so much about the mistakes and mishaps of life that we all have experienced, as much as it is about the Father's love for us. Child of God, know that *"you are the Father's Kiss"* and the world around you, family, friends, members of your church, and co-workers need to be *"kissed"* by the grace and embrace of God that is in and upon your life.

Paul says to the Colossian church in chapter 1:37, *"He decided to make known to them His **blessing to the nations**; the glorious riches of this mystery is the indwelling of **the Anointed in you!** The very hope of glory"* (The Voice Translation). You are that *blessing* to the nations! As a blessing to the nations, "go and make disciples" of *The Father's Kiss* (Matthew 28:19-20 King James Version), and the nations will thank you.

For more information about The Father's Kiss, visit us on the web at www.thefatherskiss.com or email us at info@thefatherskiss.com

Additional Publications By Dr. Cruell

The Leaders Character is a book written from Biblical principles for the natural world in which we live. A principle contained is defined as *"a universal law that is **true** in any context, situation or organization."* Truth is simply principles that are true in the church, in the military, on the college campus or in whatever organizational setting we may be a part of. Jesus said in John 8:32, *"and you shall know the truth, and the truth shall make you free."*

The Leaders Capabilities focuses on a *"Pursuit of the Future."* Capabilities can be defined as qualities or potential that can be developed. It is by pursuing future capabilities that we discover that it's never too late to learn what we are capable of.

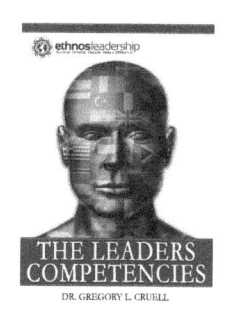

At the core of The Leaders Competencies is the idea that *"The Investment is Worth It."* The competent leader is on a never-ending quest of proficiency and mastery of his or her profession for the sake of mentoring others. It is this drive and motivation that has proven to be the key to personal and organizational legacy.

For more information about Ethnos Leadership, visit us on the web at www.ethnosleadership.com or email us at info@ethnosleadership.com.